CONFRONTING
HOMOPHOBIA
in the Black Church

AN ANALYSIS AND GUIDE

DR. BILL BURWELL JR.

Author of *ShoNuff: Confronting the Controversies*

TOWNSEND**PRESS**

SUNDAY SCHOOL PUBLISHING BOARD

330 CHARLOTTE AVENUE | NASHVILLE, TN 37201-1188

Official Publisher for the National Baptist Convention, USA, Inc.

ISBN: 978-1-939225-54-2

Printed in the United States of America
23 22 21 20 19 18 17 16 15 — 10 9 8 7 6 5 4 3 2 1

Dedicated to the New Horizons Students

NEW HOPE MISSIONARY BAPTIST CHURCH

Knoxville, Tennessee

Contents

Contents

Preface

One of the age-old lessons of life and one accentuated in the Scriptures is the fact that none of us is an island, living to ourselves alone. Therefore anything produced by those of us who are privileged to serve the kingdom of God as writers is not done in isolation from the fellowship of God's Spirit and God's people.

Even though I had addressed the subject of homosexuality in my first book, I did so with the detachment of an academician rather than as a minister giving counsel. As such, I must acknowledge that it was the students in a class I was led to create at the local church where I now serve that are responsible for rekindling my interest. They asked me, "What does the Bible say about homosexuality? Is it true that homosexuals are going to hell?"

Their query made me aware of the dilemma that we as Bible-believing ministers face in confronting this issue. Even though I was confident that the Bible condemns homosexuality as a sin, I was equally confident that the Bible does not cite it as an unforgivable sin. Yet, I was not comfortable giving them an answer that would suggest my approval of the homosexual lifestyle. In an effort to be both true to the Scriptures and yet not condone the lifestyle, I decided to prayerfully revisit the subject.

I was first led to do a self-examination, which led me to the recognition of my own prejudices and presuppositions. In so doing I was reminded that my attitude toward homosexuality was rooted primarily in the folklore of the black community which, in large part, ran contrary to the teachings of the Bible, the findings of science, and the testimony of an increasingly large number of individuals who claim to have been "born gay."

At the conclusion of my research, I realized that I could not avoid the responsibility that I as a *"steward of the mysteries of the kingdom"* had: to share my findings in the hope that they would be instructional for other stewards in their ministries.

~ DR. BILL BURWELL JR.

Acknowledgments

Among the many individuals who contributed to this work, I want to acknowledge the encouragement and contributions of my wife, Kathy, whose experiences with the gay community in Hollywood, California, where she grew up, sensitized me to the plight and pain of those caught up in the gay lifestyle.

I want to also acknowledge the contributions of my buddy here in Knoxville, Dr. Marvin Bodley, who shared his story with me. I want to extend my gratitude to Mr. Robert Boyd, who graciously edited the manuscript. I want to thank my little brother and understudy, Chico Dupas, who served as the statistician in the survey. I want to acknowledge the contributions of both my brother Ben Starks and my uncle Sonny Gooden for their storytelling in helping me to recall our childhood and our neighborhood where both the presence and practice of homosexuality was accepted as part of the norm.

Lastly, I want to extend my heartfelt gratitude to my pastor, Dr. Joe B. Maddox, who more than any other continuously encourages me to exercise my gift of writing. Even though he is not yet fully persuaded of my conclusion, his input has proved invaluable in helping me to determine how to approach this delicate subject.

Above all, I acknowledge the Spirit of Truth and trust Him to guide us into all truth, as our Lord promised He would (John 16:13).

Introduction

The LGBT (lesbian, gay, bisexual, and transgender) movement has literally exploded onto the scene. Its acceptance, growth, and victories at the ballot box, in the courts, and, most importantly, in the court of public opinion have been nothing less than phenomenal. In terms of social movements, few movements in history have accomplished so much in such a relatively short period of time. It has not simply impacted but has literally transformed the face of American culture and society.

The movement's success is nowhere more evident than in the world of entertainment and professional sports, where coming out of the closet as gay is not only accepted but also hailed as heroic. On an almost daily basis, the leading story in the news is yet another announcement of some athlete in machismo sports like football and boxing coming out acknowledging and announcing his/her homosexuality. In so doing, most of them talk about the pain and frustration they have experienced in their efforts to deny their true sexuality. They say that their homosexuality is not a choice but constitutional; they were born that way!

These claims have revived the age-old controversy of whether homosexuality is caused by genetics or environment. And once again, as has happened so often in American history, the motion picture industry is serving as somewhat of a crystal ball, predicting the future outcome of societal ills by dramatizing them on the screen. For example, the issues of segregation and racism were addressed and the outcome predicted in the film *Guess Who's Coming to Dinner?* (1967; starring Sidney Poitier, Katharine Hepburn, among others) long before society accepted and legalized interracial marriage.

Even as those in the church, courts, science, and other areas debate the issue of whether or not a person can be born gay, clearly the motion picture industry has moved beyond that debate. For they not only have accepted the claim of the LGBT movement that homosexuality is constitutional, but are now promoting the idea. Interestingly, though, they show a difference between the responses of the white community and the black community.

Two of the most popular television series this year are *Scandal* and *Empire;* both address the issue of homosexuality. The first, *Scandal,* represents the white community's response, while *Empire* reflects the black community's response.

The series *Scandal* involves the White House chief of staff, Cyrus. His homosexuality is portrayed as being constitutional, because in spite of his early efforts at denial, he could not escape its reality. As an ambitious politician in the 1980s, when gays were still in the closet, he gets married to a female as per the norm. However, because he was gay, for sixteen years he lives a promiscuous bisexual life until his wife confronts and divorces him. Twenty years later, however, he is openly gay and his same-sex marriage ceremony is performed in the rose garden on the grounds of the White House. Both he and his newlywed partner are portrayed as being constitutional gays who have pursued their lifestyle in spite of pain and rejection from parents and peers. The conclusion projected here is twofold: first, we see that the character Cyrus is now happy with his sexuality because he has accepted himself as a homosexual; second, we are shown that same-sex marriage is now both accepted and the law of the land. This again is a reflection of the white community's response to homosexuality.

The series *Empire* was written, produced, directed, and performed by African Americans. It focuses on the main character, Lucious Lyon, a rap music mogul, whose middle son, Jamal, as a toddler is seen dressing up like a girl, wearing his mother's high-heel shoes. Lucious, a macho male, finds his son's behavior disgraceful and repugnant and tries to physically beat the "sissy" out of him. Yet, in spite of the beatings, little Jamal continues to act like a girl. His behavior so enrages his father until one night, in a fit of rage and frustration, he takes little Jamal and stuffs him into a trash can and, were it not for the rescue of the mother, might have killed him.

This mirrors the response of the black community, which shows that, unlike the white community, homosexuality in the black community is an ongoing conflict and not yet accepted. It is my position that we in the black church are like Lucious, the father in the television series. Like him, we are confronted with a conflict between our firmly held belief that "a person cannot be born gay" and the reality of constitutional gays like Jamal in our families and our communities.

Even more compelling is the recently aired interview of Bruce Jenner by ABC's Diane Sawyer (aired on ABC May 24, 2015). Bruce Jenner, an acclaimed national sports hero, Olympic gold medalist, successful actor, husband, and father of six—the face of American manhood—shockingly came out and announced that he was "transgender." The two-hour interview was watched by an estimated 16.9 million viewers (*Entertainment Weekly,* May 2015), making it the most-watched program on nationwide television. In the interview Jenner declared, "My brain is much more female than male." He says that he lived as a man on the outside, but inside he was always a woman. Recently, he was featured on the cover of *Glamour Magazine* as Caitlyn—completely transgendered (*Glamour Magazine,* June 2015). I will discuss the term *transgender* and how it is distinguished from other gays later.

I point it out here along with the other television series to emphasize the growing evidence of the difficulty of the claim that a person cannot be born gay, and the necessity of the church to reexamine her position. Before proceeding any further, let me here state plainly my position on the question of whether or not a person can be born gay.

It is my belief that the overwhelming majority, as many as 90 percent of practicing homosexuals, are gay by choice or circumstances. On the other hand, I believe that the remaining 10 percent are individuals who are constitutionally gay–that is, they were born gay. Moreover, it is my belief that the failure of the church to acknowledge the 10 percent has made us homophobic and closed the door for ministry to the 90 percent, mostly young, who though not born gay, are seeking answers for the conflicting feelings of being sexually attracted to those of the same sex.

For years I have chided us for our violation of *The Law of Non-contradiction.* It states that "two opposite statements cannot both be true." In other words, we cannot on the one hand ascribe to the idea that a person cannot be born gay, and on the other hand, acknowledge that we knew someone who was. At the urging of my pastor, Dr. Joe B. Maddox, I decided to conduct a survey among some of the black Baptist churches where I have ministered to give statistical credence to the above assertion. I will share the details of this survey later in this study.

As suspected though, it confirms that we as a community have lived comfortably and callously with this self-evident contradiction for two reasons. First, it is because the gays were in the closet and not considered a threat or danger to anyone but themselves. Second, and even more importantly, it is because as Christians we cannot reconcile the reality of gays with our biblical beliefs, expressed in the words of my uncle Sonny Gooden, who serves as a deacon at my home church (Galilee Baptist Church, Birmingham, Alabama): "God don't make mistakes!"

In other words, gays are a mistake and therefore cannot be from God. The same line of thinking is expressed by others who say that God would not make something such as a homosexual, and then declare it to be an abomination (see Leviticus 20:13). My uncle and other well-meaning brethren are afraid to acknowledge the possibility of someone being constitutional gay because they think to do so would be to indict God and contradict the Bible.

Times have changed however, as gays not only have come out of the closet but are also threatening to take over the entire household. The courts of public opinion and, increasingly, the legal courts, state legislatures, and, most recently, the Supreme Court of the United States are all expressing opinions and enacting laws that support, if not endorse, the claims of the LGBT community. At the time of this writing, it appears that same-sex marriages will undeniably soon become the law of the land.

Even more troubling, however, is the fact that the church community worldwide as well as many in our own National Baptist community are divided on the issue. Statistics that I will provide later show that an increasingly larger number of individual Christians, local churches, and even entire denominations are declaring themselves as "gay-affirming."

We need look no further back than a few months ago for proof of this internal division. Dr. Forrest Harris, the president of our own denominational school American Baptist College in Nashville, Tennessee, invited a married lesbian bishop, Yvette Flunder, to speak at the 58th session of the prestigious Garnett–Britt Lecture Series. This invitation drew nationwide uproars from pastors objecting to the invitation, claiming that it violated the beliefs of our school, churches, and convention. The uproars ended with a press conference attended by a group of concerned pastors in Nashville. No actions were taken and the program proceeded as planned. Interestingly, one of the pastors at the press conference raised the question, "Who are the true owners of the school?"

In response to this question, the Board of Directors of the National Baptist Convention, USA, Inc. has come forward to claim ownership; and as such, the actions of the president of the school are answerable to them. Dr. Harris is threatening legal action and, as of this writing, the matter is unresolved.

In light of all that has been presented above, what should we in the National Baptist church community do in the face of these developments? *The Scriptures clearly teach that homosexuality is a sin and that marriage is to be between a man and a woman.* So how do we maintain our submission and loyalty to the authority of the Scriptures without appearing blind and insensitive to the tide of social change and thus irrelevant to this generation?

Summarily speaking, first and foremost, we must examine closely the basis for the thesis that *a person cannot be born gay.* In so doing, we must acknowledge the contradiction between such a claim, the growing evidence before us, and, most of all, the reality of individuals in our own families and communities whom we all agree were born gay. Only by acknowledging the possibility of such can we begin to reach the increasing number of young blacks, in our families and churches, especially in our music ministries, who are openly and defiantly practicing the gay lifestyle.

Allow me to repeat what I stated above: *our dogmatism against the possibility of one's being constitutional gay closes the door of communication not only to the few who may have been born gay but, more importantly, to the majority who were not.* Our children were taught by us and our churches that a person cannot be born gay. However, their reality, the world in which they live outside of the home and the church, contradicts what they have been taught.

First, they have acquaintances, friends, and sometimes even relatives who are openly gay. Second, the schools are teaching them that *tolerance and acceptance* are the greatest of all virtues. Specifically, they are taught not to discriminate against anyone because of their differences, and that to do so constitutes bullying, which is both unethical and illegal. Among the differences they are taught to accept are those students who appear to be (or are) openly gay. School-approved gay clubs are now coexisting alongside other fraternities (Trevor Project, West Hollywood, California).

Adding to all of this is the reality of puberty that entails both physical and emotional changes. They are as confused and curious about their emotional changes as they are about their physical changes. They need guidance and assistance with these emotional changes as well as the physical. Just as we help them with their physical growth, we need to provide avenues of help for their emotional growth. Emotions of sexual attractions are among these changes, and sometimes, these attractions can be for individuals of the same sex. Such feelings can easily lead one to ask, "Am I gay?" Rather than coming to their parents or the church whom they perceive to be closed-minded, they look for answers elsewhere.

In this day of the social media, most of them quickly turn to their phones and with a mere click they find answers to their questions. Most of these answers, however, are not just untrue but, most importantly, are unbiblical. Nevertheless, nurtured by the virtues of tolerance and acceptance in the schools, these answers fit more comfortably in their world than does the teaching they received at home and in church. They find the LGBT community to be part of the norm and reject what they see as homophobia in the church. For while we are refusing to confront the issue, the LGBT community is standing by with welcome arms, inviting them to social functions providing them with false affirmations that these feelings they are experiencing mean that they were born gay and that they should simply accept it as normal.

Second, we must respond to the pro-gay writers who claim "the Bible knows no sex ethic, only a love ethic, and thus sex between two consenting adults is not a sin" (Pamela Young, *Feminist Theology*). Our refusal to actively refute this claim has given impetus to the LGBT movement whose success is evidenced by the growing number of churches and individuals who are now "gay-affirming." Moreover, it is giving credence to those within the church, like the lesbian bishop lecturer at American Baptist College who maintains that one can be both a Christian and a practicing homosexual.

Third, we must acquaint ourselves with the multiplicity of scientific studies that have been conducted on the causes of homosexuality and note that there is no consensus among scientists as to why a person develops a particular sexual orientation. The preponderance of evidence has led many to believe that both nature and nurture—that is, a combination of genetic, hormonal, and environmental influences—factor into the cause of sexual orientation ("*Sexual Orientation, Homosexuality and Bisexuality*" Archives of the American Psychological Association, August 8, 2013).

Finally, and most importantly, I argue theologically that *the true cause of homosexuality is neither genetic nor social but sin. It is my firm conviction that sin has invaded and perverted every aspect of human existence, including the behavior of chromosomes in the prenatal stage of birth. As such, the unnatural behavior of chromosomes results in the unnatural production of homosexual births.*

The Bible teaches that all truth is of the sovereign God, but sin and Satan pervert the truth of God into a lie. Heterosexuality is God's order for human sexuality set up in the beginning; but God's order has been perverted into homosexuality, being propagated by the LGBT as being nothing more than a departure from the norm, but nevertheless from God.

It is this kind of faulty reasoning reflected by the world that labels hurricanes, tsunamis, earthquakes, and so forth, as "natural disasters" or "acts of God." Such physical disasters are not acts of God but, rather, they are the products of Satan and sin. Of course all events occur by the will of God, but some reflect the permissive will of God rather than the perfect will of God. Homosexual births, like other disasters, occur by the permissive but not the perfect will of God.

Let us take courage nevertheless in the knowledge that "where sin abounds, grace does much more." As such, we must confront homosexuality like all other sins—with the confidence that the blood of the Lamb can cleanse from all unrighteousness.

I close this book with a couple of anecdotes from my own life to illustrate the evolution of my position and how by the grace of God I am being delivered from my homophobia. I have written this book fully cognizant that my conclusions are, at best, unsettling to most, and unacceptable to others. Nevertheless, it is my belief that we can rely on the promise of our Lord, that the Holy Spirit, the Spirit of Truth, will guide us into all truth. He will guide us into the truth about this also.

CHAPTER

1

Homosexuality

What does it mean to be lesbian, gay, bisexual, or transgender?

The first difficulty one encounters in the study of this topic rests with the challenge of defining the terms. The term *gay* originated from the Old French word *gai,* which means "merry" or "full of joy." Other definitions included "carefree" and "bright and showy." Later on, the definition *carefree* expanded to mean someone who was carefree with regard to morals. This later was applied to homosexuals and prostitutes. With that strict definition, the term refers to *same-sex encounters that are marked by a carefree attitude.*

Of course there are many in the gay community who would take serious issue with this definition because of the term *carefree.* They would point out that the carefree lifestyle of gays portrayed in the media is reflective of a relatively small percentage of their community. Gay marriages they contend are as monogamous as are heterosexual marriages with no less or more faithfulness to their partners as is the case with heterosexual couples. Surveys on gay couples seem to bear out their claim. The surveys conducted indicate that separation and divorce rates among homosexual couples are about the same as the percentage of those among heterosexual couples. These numbers are susceptible to change with the legalization of gay marriage, as this will provide a paper trail that will allow for greater accuracy in gathering statistics on separation and divorce.

Others would claim that one may be considered gay or homosexual based upon the number of times one engaged in the act. It would not include those who experimented with same-sex once or twice but, rather, those who have had same sex more than five times and those who have adopted same-sex as a lifestyle. This would be true irrespective of whether the relationship was monogamous or not, as long as it involved sex between those of the same gender.

Historically speaking, the term *homosexuality* did not exist until K. M. Benkert coined it in 1869. Its popular usage dates back, perhaps, to one of the earliest studies, done by Alfred Kinsey in 1948, "Sexual Behavior in Human Males," wherein he defined as gay "any male who has had sexual intercourse with a member of the same sex." With this definition, he said that 10 percent of American men "were predominantly homosexual between the ages of 16 and 55."

John Money of John Hopkins University, a well-known sex researcher, says that although the term only gained popular usage in the nineteenth century, the phenomenon has existed probably as long as humans have walked the earth. He goes on to say that the many enigmas of sexual orientation have baffled people for centuries—including what makes children grow up to be homosexual, while others become heterosexual or bisexual, and to what degree is gender identity determined before birth—and continues to do so. Money defined *homosexual* as one who had six or more sexual experiences with members of the same sex. Using this definition, he found that 13 percent of adult males were gay and about 7 percent of adult females were lesbians (Money, 1988).

WHAT DOES IT MEAN TO BE BISEXUAL?

The term *bisexuality* can prove difficult to define because like the term *gay* it involves factors like identity, behavior, attractions, or some combination of these. *Wikipedia Encyclopedia* defines it as "sexual attraction or sexual behavior towards both males and females." It is linked with the terms gay, lesbian, and transgender, indicating its relationship to the heterosexual-homosexual continuum. When viewed on such a continuum with same-sex attractions on one end and other-sex attractions on the other end, bisexuality falls somewhere in the middle.

The Bisexual Resource Center (Boston, Massachusetts), the oldest and largest organization in the U.S., says in its mission statement that they use the term *bisexual* "as an umbrella term for people who recognize and honor their potential for sexual and emotional attraction to more than one gender." They see themselves distinctive from, but yet as part of, the wider LGBT community, fostering acceptance socially and politically.

LIVING ON THE DOWN-LOW (DL)

The presence of bisexual men in the African-American community who identified themselves as heterosexual but were secretly having sex with other men gave rise to the term *down-low*. The term was popularized by J. L. King, a black man who appeared on the *Oprah Winfrey Show* promoting his biographical account of his life as a bisexual. He discussed how he grew up trying to please his military father, who demanded that his sons act like men. Yet he says that as early as age ten he found himself attracted to boys. In spite of his feelings, though, he lived the life of a happily married heterosexual with a family until he was caught by his wife.

Interestingly, J. L. King does not consider himself gay and does not participate in the activities of the LGBT movement. To do so, he says, would be putting a label on himself simply for the comfort of others. Three other bisexual black men followed King's appearance on *Oprah,* and they, like King, do not identify with or openly participate in the LGBT movement. For them, however, their reasons are simply that their double lives must be kept secret for their sakes and/or for the welfare of their families, as many of these brothers are married.

WHAT DOES IT MEAN TO BE LESBIAN?

Lesbianism may be simply defined as "female homosexuality" or "one who experiences romantic love or sexual attraction to other females" (*Merriam-Webster's Dictionary*). The term *lesbian* is a twentieth-century construct popularized by the rise of the LGBT movement to distinguish homosexual women from homosexual men.

Like the other terms in the LGBT community, the definition of just what the term *lesbian* means is controversial. Some contend that "sexual desire" is the major component of the definition while others who engage in same-sex reject not only identifying as lesbians, but also as "bisexual" while other women's self-identification as lesbian may not align with their sexual orientation or sexual behavior. Sexual identity is not necessarily the same as one's sexual orientation or sexual behavior due to various reasons, such as the fear of identifying with their sexual orientation in a homophobic society (*Wikipedia Encyclopedia*).

WHAT DOES IT MEAN TO BE TRANSGENDER?

Of the four terms in LGBT, the last one may prove the most difficult to define primarily because it may encompass any of the previous terms. *Transgender* is independent of sexual orientation and may include people who identify as heterosexual, homosexual, bisexual, etc. *Transgender* may be defined as "the state of one's gender identity or expression not matching one's assigned sex" (GLADD–Transgender glossary, USA, May 2010). Or, "a person whose identity does not conform unambiguously to conventional notions of male or female gender, but combines or moves between these" (*Oxford English Dictionary*).

With reference to the continuum between heterosexuality and homo-sexuality, a transgender individual may have characteristics that are normally associated with a particular gender and identify elsewhere on the traditional gender continuum, or even exist outside of the continuum. Transgender may also identify as "bi-gender," "pan-gender," or along several places on either the traditional gender continuum or the more encompassing continuums that have been developed in responses to recent significantly more detailed studies (Layton).

The much-watched ABC interview of Bruce Jenner cited earlier ushered the term *transgender* into the living rooms, psyche, and conversation of American households and, because of the passion with which it was presented, raised the overarching question, "Was he born like that?"

Until the twenty-first century, gender identity was thought of as being entirely a social construct, with most of our gender formation occurring between the ages of 1 and 4. The general thought now, however, is that gender identity is programmed at birth, although social factors can potentially overwhelm this programming ("The Transgender Brain," Transas City).

The common phrase "all babies start out female, and it's only later that they become male" is partially true. In fact, the influence of testosterone on a fetus has been described as a *defeminization* process, changing a fetus that was essentially predestined to be female into male (Gooren, 2006). Testosterone production and the conversion of some testosterone to dihydrotesterone between weeks 6 and 12 of pregnancy are critical to the initial development of male features, such as the penis, prostate gland, and scrotum. In the absence of these male hormones, female genitalia develop instead (Bao, 2011).

Brain development, however, does not occur until the second half of the pregnancy term, after the genitals have developed, and the continued presence of male hormones result in a brain that has subtle, but critical physical differences from the female brain. The fact that the brain and the genitals develop at different times in the womb means that a misalignment between the genitals and brain may develop, leading to either an intersex condition, or a transgender individual (Bao, 2011).

It should be noted, however, that in spite of the wide range and an increasingly large number of scientific studies done on the brains of transgenders, none have concluded definitively that there is a distinct difference between the brains of heterosexuals and homosexuals either in the prenatal stage or at birth. The evidence, however, as will be pointed out in other studies, suggests that much more research is needed.

OTHER RELATED TERMS

(Source: GLADD Media Reference Guide Transgender Issues)

SEX – The classification of people as male or female based upon the appearance of their external anatomy. A person's sex is actually a combination of bodily characteristics including chromosomes, hormones, internal and external reproductive organs, and secondary sex characteristics.

GENDER IDENTITY – One's internal, deeply held sense of his/her gender. For transgender people, their own internal gender identity does not match the sex they were assigned at birth.

GENDER EXPRESSION – External manifestations of gender, expressed through one's name, pronouns, clothing, haircut, behavior, voice, or bodily characteristics. Society identifies these cues as masculine or feminine, although what is considered masculine or feminine changes over time and varies by culture. Typically, transgender people seek to make their gender expression align with their gender identity rather than with the sex they were assigned at birth.

SEXUAL ORIENTATION – Describes an individual's enduring physical, romantic, and/or emotional attraction to another person. Gender identity and sexual orientation are not the same. Transgender people may be straight, lesbian, gay, or bisexual.

CROSS-DRESSER – Heterosexual men who occasionally wear clothes, makeup, and accessories culturally associated with women. This activity is a form of gender expression not done solely for entertainment purposes but as a source of emotional and sexual gratification. Cross-dressers typically do not wish to permanently change their sex or live full-time as women.

CHAPTER

2

How Widespread Is Homosexuality?

It is difficult, if not impossible, to know just how widespread homosexuality is in the United States partly because of the difficulty in defining the term and partly because of the stigma attached to it. Nevertheless, a number of studies have been conducted over the years that provide some estimates.

The oldest and most often quoted study on the prevalence of homosexuality was reported in the studies of Alfred Kinsey, *Sexual Behavior in the Human Male* (1948) and *Sexual Behavior in the Human Female* (1953) which reported that

- 37 percent of males and 13 percent of females had at least some overt homosexual experience to orgasm.
- 10 percent of males were more or less exclusively homosexual and 8 percent of males were exclusively homosexual for at least three years between the ages of 16 and 55. For females, Kinsey reported a range of 2 to 6 percent for more or less exclusively homosexual experience response.
- 4 percent of males and 1 to 3 percent of females had been exclusively homosexual after the onset of adolescence up to the time of the interview.
- Kinsey devised a classification scheme to measure sexual orientation. It is called the Kinsey Scale.

In a later survey Hunt (1974) adjusted Kinsey's 37 percent survey (for males having had some same-sex contact to orgasm) to 255 *and* Kinsey's 4 percent exclusive homosexuality figure for males to 2 to 3 percent. He considered less than 1 percent of females as "mainly to completely homosexual." The Kinsey Report has generally put the percentage of practicing homosexuals at 10 percent of the U.S. population.

However, this estimate has been challenged in a report in *The Washington Post* with the headline, "CDC: Nation's Percentage of Gays, Lesbians, Bisexuals Less than Supposed." It reports that a highly definitive study from 2013 has put the size of the gay population in the United States at far less than previously reported.

The National Health Interview Survey by the Centers for Disease Control and Prevention, which provides the federal government's most relied upon estimate of the nation's health behaviors, found that fewer than 3 percent of respondents self-identified as gay, lesbian, or bisexual. Only 1.6 percent of respondents self-identified as gay or lesbian, and even less, 0.7 percent, self-identified as bisexual.

WHO ARE THE LGBT?

The stereotypical image of the LGBT population is depicted on the television screens as white, male, urban, and wealthy, as in the award-winning series *Modern Family,* is now being challenged by a recent Gallup poll in which it interviewed 121,000 people—the largest study of its kind, they claim.

Their findings estimate that of the 3.4 percent of American adults who identify as lesbian, gay, bisexual, or transgender, 4.6 percent of the LGBT population are African Americans. According to demographer Gary Gates, the report's lead author, the LGBT community has a higher proportion of nonwhite people and clearly is not overly wealthy (Gallup Poll, Gary Gates, Princeton, NJ).

The survey was conducted between June and September 2012. It found that 4 percent of Hispanics, 4.3 percent of Asians, and 3.2 percent of nonwhites consider themselves part of the LGBT community.

The survey found that there was a slight gender difference: 3.6 percent of females identified as LGBT, compared to 3.3 percent of men. Younger adults aged 18 to 29 were more likely than their elders to identify as LGBT. However, among those aged 18 to 29, 8.3 percent of women identified as LGBT, compared with 4.6 percent of men the same age.

In contrast to some previous smaller studies, the Gallup survey found that identification as LGBT was highest among Americans with the lowest levels of education.

As stated in the introduction, the presence of homosexuality in the African-American community has never been denied. Throughout our history, from the pulpits to the political arena black homosexuals have played prominent roles. From my own personal experiences in the Civil Rights Movement dating back to the 1950s, two of the most noted activists, James Baldwin and Bayard Rustin, were both openly gay. However, there has never been such widespread acknowledgment and acceptance of gays as it is today. There is even a group, "blaquebigayministers," which was founded by Church of God in Christ (COGIC) Elder Ronald Kimbre, boasting 787 members since July 2000. This gay organization says on its Yahoo! Web site, "WELCOME: This fellowship is for support and encouragement especially of Black Christian ministers & friends who are *family* (bi- or same-gender loving) and need a place of refuge" (Tag Archives: blaquebigayministers).

Indeed, the LGBT movement is widespread across religious, ethnic, racial, and socioeconomic ranks.

CHAPTER

3

How Widespread Is Homosexuality in the Christian Church?

Data on the number of Christians who identify themselves as homosexual in the general Christian community is hard to come by for a number of reasons, but mostly because of the stigma attached to it by the church. According to data from the National Council of Churches (*Yearbook*, 2011), there is the conservative estimate that 3.5 percent of the 231 million Americans who identify themselves as Christian also identify as gay. Using these figures there is an estimated gay population of 8 million Christians in the United States.

GAY-AFFIRMING CHURCHES BY DENOMINATION

The largest number of these individuals can be found in gay-affirming churches. The statistics from GayChurch.org in its "2013 Gay Affirming Church Survey" report that there are now 4,623 gay-affirming churches in the U.S.A. and abroad. More than 70 percent of these churches come from what they refer to as "The Big Five" denominations, consisting of United Church of Christ, Episcopal Lutheran ELCA, Presbyterian, and United Methodist. The United Church of Christ is the most prolific gay-affirming denomination in the world but only slightly ahead of Episcopal churches.

To that end, gay-affirming churches encompass seventy-two different denominations that span across forty-six different countries. Gay and lesbian churches are only outnumbered by the Roman Catholic Church (68 million) and the Southern Baptist Convention (16 million).

Their survey also reports that the number of independent churches now surpasses the number of Roman Catholic parishes that are publicly pronouncing their affirming stance. The top fourteen gay-affirming denominations and the number of their churches include Non-denominational (372), Independent

Catholic (265), Roman Catholic (244), United Church of Canada (192), Metropolitan Community Church (187), Disciples of Christ (183), Anglican (168), American Baptist (164), and Quaker (130).

In a summarizing statement the group states, "The gay-affirming revival within the Christian churches continues to expand at a rapid rate. Numbers aside, we are seeing a continuation of a 'grassroots' effort which propels the leading edge of this revival: individual pastors, congregants, families, friends, and countless others who are at the heart of this movement."

CHRISTIAN DENOMINATIONAL STATEMENTS ON LGBT

The traditional churches have responded by issuing doctrinal statements reflecting their doctrinal view on homosexuality as a sin, while at the same time urging the availability of repentance and redemption:

ROMAN CATHOLICISM

Inasmuch as the Christian church is rooted historically in Roman Catholicism, it seems best to begin with an examination of the position taken by the Roman Catholic Church excerpted from their official statement.

"Generally speaking, the Roman Catholic Church considers human sexual behavior that it sees as properly expressed to be sacred, *sacramental* in nature. Sexual acts other than *unprotected* vaginal intercourse within a heterosexual marriage are considered sinful because in the Church's understanding, sexual acts, by their nature, are meant to be both unitive and procreative (mirroring God's inner Trinitarian life). The church also understands the complementarity of the sexes to be part of God's plan. Same-gender sexual acts are incompatible with this framework."

"Homosexual acts are contrary to the natural law. They close the sexual act to the gift of life. They do not proceed from a genuine affective and sexual complementarity. Under no circumstances can they be approved."

These teachings are, of course, not limited to the issue of homosexuality, but are also the general background for the Catholic prohibitions against, for example, fornication, contraception, pornography, consummated anal sex, masturbation, and all other forms of non-coital sex.

The Church, though, in seeking "social justice" has clearly stated that homosexual desires or attractions themselves are not necessarily sinful. They are said to be *disordered* in the sense that they tempt one to do something that is sinful (i.e., the homosexual act), but temptations beyond one's control are not considered sinful in and of themselves. For this reason, while the church does oppose same-gender sexual acts, it also officially urges respect and love for those who do experience same-sex attractions and isn't opposed to the homosexual orientation, thus the Catholic Church is also opposed to persecutions and violence against the LGBT community.

"The number of men and women who have deep-seated homosexual tendencies is not negligible. This inclination, which is objectively disordered, constitutes for most of them a trial. They must be accepted with respect, compassion, and sensitivity. Every sign of unjust discrimination in their regard should be avoided. These persons are called to fulfill God's will in their lives and, if they are Christians, to unite to the sacrifice of the Lord's Cross the difficulties they may encounter from their condition."

The Church considers the call to chastity universal to all persons according to their state in life. For those who do experience gay sexual attractions, the Catholic Church offers the following counsel:

"Homosexual persons are called to chastity. By the virtues of self-mastery that teach them inner freedom, at times by the support of disinterested friendship, by prayer and sacramental grace, they can and should gradually and resolutely approach Christian perfection."

SOUTHERN BAPTISTS

The Southern Baptist Convention, the largest of the Baptist denominations and the largest Protestant group in the U.S., considers same-gender sexual behavior to be sinful, stating clearly that its' members "affirm God's plan for marriage and sexual intimacy—one man, and one woman, for life. Homosexuality is not a valid alternative lifestyle. The Bible condemns it as a sin. It is not, however, an unforgivable sin. The same redemption available to all sinners is available to homosexuals. They, too, may become new creations in Christ."

AMERICAN BAPTISTS

The American Baptist Churches, USA, officially regards homosexual conduct "as incompatible with Biblical teaching."

THE ASSOCIATION OF WELCOMING BAPTISTS

This rather small group of some fifty churches and organizations is committed to the "full inclusion" of gay and lesbian persons in their congregations.

THE PROTESTANT EPISCOPAL CHURCH, USA

The PECUSA, which considers itself to be both Protestant and Catholic, is considered the nation's fourteenth-largest denomination, largely known for its liberality and a major supporter of the Civil Rights Movement in the USA. The General Assembly has passed resolutions that allow for same-sex marriages in states where it is legal. It has also called for the full civil equality of gay and lesbian couples, including the ordination of gay and lesbian priests. The convention has gone so far as to develop an official liturgy to bless same-sex marriages.

LUTHERANISM

The Evangelical Lutheran Church in America, the largest Lutheran church body in the United States as of August 21, 2009, voted in favor of allowing non-celibate gays to become ordained ministers. They also voted against a measure that would have allowed non-celibate gay ordination and the blessing of same-sex unions. Lutheran policy states that LGBT are welcomed and encouraged to become members and participate in the life of the congregation.

THE UNITED METHODIST CHURCH

Since 1972, The UMC in its official positions on homosexuality has maintained the *Book of Discipline* and has declared "homosexual practice" to be "incompatible with Christian teaching." Following the 1972 incompatible clause, it has added additional restrictions at subsequent General Conferences. Currently, The UMC prohibits the ordination of "practicing self-avowed homosexuals," forbids clergy from blessing or presiding over same-sex unions, forbids the use of UMC facilities for same-sex union ceremonies, and prohibits the use of church funds for "gay caucuses" or other groups that "promote the acceptance of homosexuality."

PENTECOSTALISM

Most churches that are within the Pentecostal Movement view homosexual behavior as sinful. The Assemblies of God, second-largest Pentecostal church in the U.S.A., makes its view on homosexuality clear in a position paper, stating, "It should be noted at the outset that there is absolutely no affirmation of homosexual behavior found anywhere in Scripture. Rather, the consistent sexual ideal is chastity for those outside a monogamous heterosexual marriage and fidelity for those inside such a marriage. There is also abundant evidence that homosexual behavior, along with illicit heterosexual behavior, is immoral and comes under the judgment of God."

There are, however, a growing number of LGBT-affirming Pentecostal churches, both denominations and independents churches. These include the "Global Alliance of Affirming Apostolic Pentecostals," who affirm that their study of the Scriptures in the original languages find no condemnation of homosexuality.

THE PRESBYTERIAN CHURCH, USA

The largest body of Presbyterian churches in the U.S.A. has approved the ordination of non-celibate gays. On July 8, 2010, the General Assembly voted to propose to the General Assembly a constitutional amendment to remove the restriction against the ordination of partnered homosexuals. A year later in 2011 the majority of Presbyterians voted to approve the constitutional change.

Nevertheless, the Church remains divided over the issues of homosexuality. Although gay and lesbian persons are welcome to become members of the church denominational policy prohibited non-celibate same-sex relations (as well as non-celibate heterosexual relations outside of marriage) for those serving as ministers or as elders on key church boards in 2010. The church does bless same-sex unions, but does not officially permit same-sex marriages, and does not explicitly support the consummation of such unions.

Other smaller American Presbyterian bodies condemn same-sex sexual behavior as incompatible with biblical morality, but believe gays and lesbians can repent and abandon the lifestyle.

THE UNITED CHURCH OF CHRIST

The structure of the UCC is "congregational" rule that does not make binding on its members the recommendations of any upper level or body. Approximately 10 percent of UCC congregations have adopted an official

"Open and Affirming" statement welcoming gay and lesbian persons in all aspects of church life.

THE NATIONAL BAPTIST CONVENTION OF AMERICA AND NBC, USA

Neither of the two National Baptist Conventions, which represent the largest number of black Baptists, have issued any public statements on homosexuality. This is in keeping with their refusal to take doctrinal stances, allegedly because of their belief in the autonomy of the local church. Having taken that position to task in my former book, I shall not do so here.

CHAPTER

4

Scientific Studies on the Causes
of Homosexuality: Genetics or Socialization?

Scientists have conducted more than two dozen studies testing the hypotheses that homosexuality is genetic. Listed below in summary form are the most well-known and scientifically significant studies conducted over the past fifty years.

SWAAB & HOFMAN:

This research was a study on the volume of the suprachiasmatic nucleus (hereafter referred to as SCN) in homosexual men. The SCN is a cell group located in the basal part of the brains of mammalians. It has been thought to be a principal component of the biological clock that generates and coordinates hormonal, physiological, and behavioral body rhythms. Thus, it has been thought to have involvement in sex because of the varying body rhythms in sexual desire, as well as the sexual changes that come with aging.

The study observed the brains of thirty-four subjects. There was a reference group of eighteen male subjects who died of a variety of causes. There was a second group of ten homosexual men who died of AIDS, and a third group of six heterosexuals who died of AIDS. This last group consisted of four males and two females. The conclusion of this study is that "the human hypothalamus revealed that the volume of the . . . SCN in homosexual men is 1.7 times as large as that of the reference group of male subjects and contains 2.1 times as many cells."

In plain and simple terms, this study seems to support the long-held belief (by some) that the Adam's apples of homosexual men are larger than those of heterosexual men.

SIMON LEVAY (1991):

This study was similar to that of Hofman and Swaab's, in that it also focused upon the hypothalamus, looking specifically at the third Interstitial

Nucleus of the Anterior Hypothalamus (INAH3), a gland that is important both hormonally and sexually. LeVay's research was done on the brains of both homosexual and heterosexual men in an area of tiny neurons that is directly related to sexual response. His study reported that the INAH3 in heterosexual men was twice the size of that in homosexual men.

LeVay's conclusion seemed to corroborate the findings of Swaab and Hofman that "there is a significant difference between the hypothalamus of heterosexual and homosexual men" (LeVay, 1991).

LeVay's study received worldwide media attention and was used by some pro-gay proponents to make declarations that his study did not support. To clear up these issues, LeVay, who is openly gay, conducted an interview in 1994 in which he said, "It's important to stress what I didn't find. I did not prove that homosexuality is genetic, or find a genetic cause for being gay. I didn't show that gay men are born that way; this is the most common mistake people make in interpreting my work. Nor did I locate a gay center in the brain. The INAH3 is less likely to be the sole gay nucleus of the brain than a part of a chain of nuclei engaged in men and women's sexual behavior." (Nimmons, 1994).

GAY MEN TWIN STUDIES:

A number of studies have been conducted on gay twins in an effort to prove that homosexuality is genetic. The oldest, largest, and most prominent of these is the study conducted in 1991 by Dr. Richard C. Pillard, a psychiatry professor at Boston University School of Medicine and a colleague from Northwestern University. The study concluded that in identical twins, if one twin was gay, the other had about a 50 percent chance of also being gay. In fraternal twins, the rate was about 20 percent.

Since identical twins share their genetic makeup and fraternal twins only half, the researchers believed genes were the explanation. The more closely genetically linked a pair is, the more likely they are to exhibit similar gay or straight tendencies.

In disagreement with the conclusions of Pillard, Dr. Neil Whitehead, a scientific researcher for the New Zealand government, says, "At best genetics is a minor factor." He reasons that if homosexuality is caused by prenatal conditions and one twin is gay, the co-twin should also be gay because identical twins share the same genes or DNA. However, he says that the studies reveal something else. "If an identical twin has same-sex attraction the chances the co-twin has it are only about 11% for men and 14% for women."

He says, "No one is born gay, the predominant things that create homosexuality in one identical twin and not in the other have to be post-birth factors."

GAY GENE STUDY:

Harvard-trained Dean Hamer's 1993 announcement was big news, with what was described as the discovery of a "gay gene." The National Cancer Institute researcher found that gay brothers share a specific region of the X chromosome at a higher rate than gay men shared with straight brothers. Hamer took forty DNA samples from homosexual men and genetically examined them. He found there was a remarkable link for five genetic markers on a section of the X chromosome called Xq28. Hamer hypothesized, after examining the family trees of the same men, that on each of the subjects' mother's side there were higher numbers of homosexual men.

Although subsequent studies called into question the assertion by Hamer of the existence of a gay gene, a recent study conducted on 409 pairs of gay brothers fingers the same region on the X (*Psychological Medicine,* November 2014). Nevertheless, neither Hamer nor this latest study provides proof of the existence of specific genes that cause homosexuality.

PARENTAL MANIPULATION THEORY:

Richard Alexander, of the University of Michigan, noted for his work on natural selection and social theory, gained national attention when he extended his theories to the arena of human sexuality. He says that one or both parents are able to neuter and control offspring to promote their (the parents') evolutionary fitness, which passes the genes into the next generation. If proven true, it would mean that couples could manipulate their genes to promote or prevent either heterosexuality or homosexuality.

PLANOPHYSICAL THEORY:

This theory was the basis for the American Psychological Association classification of homosexuality as a mental disorder. It was a concept postulated by Freudian psychologist David Halpern. He believed that homosexuality is a freak of nature, an error as a result of unresolved oedipal issues. He said that a weak father and a strong mother would result in a weak homosexual son due to the mother having a stronger image (Halpern, 1990). Other psychologists have argued the opposite, however, alleging that a stronger son who is compensating for his weak father becomes stronger as a heterosexual man rather than a homosexual. The APA removed homosexuality from its list of mental illnesses and this theory is no longer seriously considered as a reliable case for homosexuality.

OPPOSITE-SEX TWINS AND ADOLESCENT SAME-SEX ATTRACTION:

In 2002, Peter Bearman from Columbia University and Hannah Bruckner from Yale studied factors related to same-sex attraction in a group of 20,745 adolescents. They found that adolescent males with an opposite-sex twin were more than twice as likely to report same-sex attraction compared to males with a male or female non-twin sibling.

Unlike studies looking at the fraternal birth order effect (FBOE) that state the more older biological brothers one has, the more likely one is to be gay, no FBOE was found in this study. Instead, Bearman and Bruckner found the opposite-sex twin effect was eliminated by the presence of an older brother. Furthermore, they found no evidence for genetic or prenatal effects. For example, the presence of a twin sister with no older brother could push family and peer life away from male-gendered activities (*American Journal of Sociology*, May 2002).

SWEAT AND URINE BRAIN STUDY OF GAY MEN:

In 2000, a group of Swedish researchers at the Karolinska Institute, Stockholm, using a brain imaging technique, reported finding differences in how the brains of straight men responded to women's urine and male sweat, both believed to be pheromones (scent-related chemicals that are key to sexual arousal in animals). When straight men smelled the female urine compound, their hypothalamus lit up. Not so with the gay men. Instead, their brains lit up when they smelled the male sweat compound.

The findings are similar to the previously cited study of Simon LeVay on that small region of the hypothalamus reported to be twice as large in straight men as in women or gay men.

Pheromones, chemicals emitted by one individual to evoke some behavior in another of the same species, are known to govern sexual activity in animals. The new research supports the existence of human pheromones (*The Proceedings of the National Academy of Sciences*, May 2005).

FRUIT FLY STUDY:

In 2005, scientists in Vienna isolated a master genetic switch for sexual orientation in fruit flies. When they flipped the switch, the genetically altered females ignored advances of males and attempted to mate with females, even doing the courting dance and song that males use.

EX-GAY STUDIES: CAN GAYS CHANGE?

Scientists continue to debate the efficacy of "Reparative therapy" as a treatment to change one's sexual orientation. In 2001, Robert Spitzer, a professor of psychiatry at Columbia University, delivered a controversial paper at the annual meeting of the APA that was later published in the *Archives of Sexual Behavior* (2003). Spitzer's findings challenge the widely held assumption that homosexual orientation is an intrinsic part of a person's identity that can never be changed. The study has attracted particular attention because its author, a prominent psychiatrist, is viewed as a historic champion of gay activism. Spitzer played a prominent role in 1973 in removing homosexuality from the American Psychiatric Association's manual of mental disorders.

His paper argued that some highly motivational people can change people from gay to straight. He conducted 200 telephone interviews with people who had already changed their sexual orientation. About 66 percent of men and 44 percent of women he interviewed had, over the course of a few years, achieved a level of "good heterosexual functioning."

His study also found that "89% of men and 95% of women said they were bothered only slightly, or not at all, by unwanted sexual feelings" but that "only 11% of the men and 37% of the women reported a complete absence of homosexual indicators, including same-sex attraction" (Robert Spitzer, *Can Some Gay Men and Lesbians Change Their Sexual Orientation?*)

Spitzer's paper angered many in the gay community, accusing him of betraying them. The APA issued an official disavowal of Spitzer's paper and other scientists have criticized the study for its sampling methods and criteria for success. In response, Spitzer admitted that "he had no way of knowing whether or not the study participants were being honest but he felt that they were being candid with him" (Ritter Martin, *The Washington Post,* May 9, 2001).

Nevertheless, this study, Spitzer concludes, "clearly goes beyond anecdotal information and provides evidence that reparative therapy is sometimes successful." Spitzer acknowledges the difficulty of assessing how many gay men and women in the general population would actually desire reparative therapy if they knew of its availability; many people, he notes, are evidently content with a gay identity and have no desire to change.

Today, both the APA and the American Medical Association are opposed to treatments to "cure" homosexuality, such as "reparative" or conversion therapy, which is based on the assumption that homosexuality per se is a mental disorder.

Conclusion

Summarizing the data of the many and varied scientific studies previously cited leads this writer to conclude that *homosexuality cannot be proven scientifically to be genetic.* In spite of the many indices that there may be a genetic component no reputable researcher claims to have proven that genes determine sexual orientation.

On the other hand, there seems to be increasing evidence that suggests that genes may play a role in determining one's *predisposition toward homosexuality and that when genes are accompanied by various social factors this may lead to homosexuality.* I continue to argue that wisdom suggests that we conclude that human sexuality, like every other aspect of human behavior in *fallen mankind apart from sin,* is influenced by both biological and societal factors.

CHAPTER

5

LGBT: The Courts and State Legislatures

Perhaps no institution in America is more indicative of the gains and strides made by the LGBT community than those gained in the courts.

THE SUPREME COURT

The Supreme Court agreed on January 15, 2015, to settle the national debate on same-sex marriage and issue its ruling before the term ended in late June. In an earlier ruling the Court decided to let stand five federal appellate court rulings that recognized a constitutional right for gay people to marry (Supremecourt.gov/opinions, June 26, 2013).

The practical effects of this non-decision are considerable. At a minimum, it means that the five states whose cases were before the court—Utah, Oklahoma, Virginia, Wisconsin, and Indiana—should allow same-sex marriage immediately. In addition, the states covered by the circuit courts that include these states will almost certainly allow same-sex marriages as well. This includes the Fourth Circuit, covering Maryland, Virginia, West Virginia, North Carolina, and South Carolina; the Seventh Circuit, including Illinois, Indiana, and Wisconsin; and the 10th District, which covers Colorado, Kansas, New Mexico, Utah, and Wyoming.

The challenge to the longstanding belief that *marriage was a legal union between a man and a woman* worked its way from a proposition (Proposition 8) in California to the United States Supreme Court, which on June 26, 2013, voted 5-4 to strike down the Defense of Marriage Act (DOMA).

The court provided the LGBT with two major victories, first by ruling that same-sex couples were entitled to federal benefits, and second, by declining to decide a case from California effectively allowing same-sex marriages there.

The rulings leave in place laws banning same-sex marriage around the nation, and the court declined to say whether there was a constitutional right to such unions. But in clearing the way for same-sex marriage in California, the nation's most populous state, the court effectively increased to 13 the number of states that allow it. About 30 percent of Americans will live in jurisdictions where it is legal. At the time of this writing, it is becoming increasingly clear that eventually same-sex marriage will become the law of the land.

The court in its ruling said that DOMA violated the rights of same-sex couples by demoting their marriages to second-class status when compared to their heterosexual peers. The court elaborating on its decision said that the law wrongly "instructs all federal officials and indeed all persons with whom same-sex couples interact, including their own children, that their marriage is less worthy than the marriages of others."

The impact of this law is incalculable because in changing the definition of marriage, from *a union between a man and a woman* to *a union between two consenting adults,* it redefines "family," the basic institution in every culture. The response to this ruling came quickly from both those who support LGBT communities and those who do not.

Representative of the LGBT community were like those of Chad Griffin, president of the Human Rights campaign, who called the ruling a "joyous milestone," adding, "Today's historic decision put two giant cracks in the dark wall of discrimination that separates committed gay and lesbian couples from full equality."

JUSTICE DEPARTMENT RECOGNIZES SAME-SEX MARRIAGES

U.S. Attorney General Eric Holder, in a speech delivered at the 14th Annual Lambda Legal Reception (June 10, 2014), announced a new policy memorandum that "directs all Justice Department employees to give lawful same-sex marriages full and equal protection, to the greatest extent possible. This means that in every courthouse, in every proceeding, and in every place where a member of the Department of Justice stands on behalf of the United States, they will strive to ensure that same-sex marriages receive the same privileges, protections, and rights as opposite-sex marriages under federal law."

Those benefits include all spousal privileges, such as couples cannot be compelled to testify against each other, should be eligible to file for bankruptcy jointly, and are entitled to the same rights and privileges as federal prison inmates in opposite-sex marriages. He went on to compare the gay rights movement to the Civil Rights Movement of the 1960s. "Fully 60 years after the Supreme Court's decision in *Brown v. Board of Education*—the LGBT community is still waiting for its own unequivocal declaration that separate is inherently unequal."

LGBT TAUGHT IN PUBLIC SCHOOLS?

As the representative of the Black Student Union at my school, California State University, Northridge (1969), I was given the responsibility of presenting the case for Black Studies as an academic discipline, which I successfully accomplished. Within months after our victory as blacks, other groups—Latinos, Asians, women, and so forth—pointed out that they, too, were minorities who were discriminated against just as were blacks and, thus, were in need of similar treatment. The result was the development of Latino, Asian, and Women Studies alongside Black Studies.

The statements of Eric Holder and others comparing the LGBT movement to the Civil Rights Movement have given impetus to the strategy to make it a requirement that gay and lesbian studies become a part of the curriculum for public schools.

Comparing the persecution of gays to that of other minority groups, the LGBT point to the increase of bullying and violence against gay students, some of which has led to an upsurge of suicide by gay teens. The curriculum would have students take lessons on issues affecting gays, lesbians, bisexuals, and transgender people, with schools granted discretion about what age to start the lessons.

After easy passage by the Senate and State Assembly, California Governor Jerry Brown signed into law the new bill requiring that public schools teach gay and lesbian history and transgender students are allowed to choose the appropriate restroom (*California Family Code Section 299*).

Could the actions of California's governor become the precedence for what is to follow in public schools across the country? Legal experts point out that if this is done, there is little anyone can do to challenge such a curriculum. The First Amendment's protection of religious freedom might not apply because it is firmly established in law that families are free to withdraw their children from public schools in favor of private schools or homeschooling.

Sex education is mandatory in secondary schools. Many primary schools also choose to teach sex education in some form. If the legal definition of marriage changes, the law will require that children learn about gay marriage as part of sex education (Damon Linker, *The Week,* February 14, 2014).

LGBT AT THE GRAMMYS 2014

One of the grandest displays of the extent to which the world of entertainment promotes and celebrates the LGBT lifestyle was plainly and powerfully on display at the 2014 Grammys telecast.

Queen Latifah, a black female artist who arose from being a rapper on the streets of New Jersey to become a successful pop artist, actress, and now host of her own television show—herself rumored to be a lesbian—officiated the live wedding of thirty-three gay and straight couples in a church-like setting, complete with a gospel choir. The ceremony was performed while rap stars Macklemore and Ryan Lewis sang "Same Love," the song dubbed as the same-sex anthem with lyrics like "If I was gay, I would think hip-hop hates me . . ." Queen said, "This song is a love song not for some of us, but for all of us. Strip away the fear, underneath it's all the same love" (*Variety,* January 26, 2014).

GAY FAMILY SITCOM ENDORSED BY FIRST FAMILY

Television, the acknowledged leader in the world of media, is perhaps the strongest indication of just how far the LGBT movement has progressed. Among the many television shows promoting the LGBT lifestyle, the most celebrated program of today is the sitcom, *Modern Family.* It depicts as *modern* a family with two men and an adopted child. This program has not only been celebrated as the most popular award-winning show on television, but also it has even received the endorsement of the First family. President Obama, in a guest appearance on a late-night show, divulged that this show was the most watched by him and his family.

PRESIDENT BARACK OBAMA ENDORSES SAME-SEX MARRIAGE

President Barack Obama reversed his previous stance against same-sex marriage, saying on ABC News that "same-sex couples should be able to get married." He becomes the first U.S. president in history to endorse gay marriage.

He attributed his change to the relationships that he had formed with the gay members of his staff. He said that after several years of close interaction with his gay staff members, many of whom were living with partners in committed, monogamous relationships, he could no longer in good conscience deny them the right to be together, and to be afforded all the rights of heterosexual couples (*USA Today,* May 10, 2012).

BOY SCOUTS OF AMERICA ORGANIZATION LIFTING BAN ON GAYS

As I am completing this manuscript, it is being reported that the Boy Scouts of America Organization is now considering lifting their policy banning gays from their ranks. So we see yet another American institution bowing to the pressure of the LGBT movement.

In addition, Ireland becomes the first country in the world to pass constitutional amendment legalizing same-sex marriage *(NBC News*, May 23, 2015).

Conclusion

More than a few times during the writing of this manuscript, I have found it needful to insert or update current statistics or the latest development on the LGBT and their gains in the arena of same-sex marriage. There seems little doubt that gays are not simply out of the closet, but are out of the house and on the march, breaking down barriers and obstacles of resistance in every strata of American society and culture and, as is seen by today's news, internationally also.

CHAPTER

6

Homosexuality and the Bible: Responses to Pro-Gay Interpretations

s we search the Scriptures on this issue, let us do so by reminding ourselves of the two questions confronting us. First, does the Bible condemn homosexuality as a sin? Second, does the Bible teach that it is a sin more grievous than all others—even unforgivable?

As is well known, the Christian community has long held to the belief that the Bible condemns homosexuality as a sin. A few have even taught that it is an unforgivable sin. In opposition to this is the claim of the LGBT community that the Bible does not condemn homosexuality primarily, they allege, because the Bible knows no "sex ethic" but only a "love ethic."

Theologians of the LGBT community furthermore accuse those who have used the Bible to condemn homosexuality as being guilty of misinterpreting Bible texts, ignoring the fact that such condemnations always occur within the context of God's condemnation of prostitution, rape, and idolatry. In contradistinction, the pro-gay writers claim that the Bible, when rightly interpreted, does not *condemn* but rather *condones* the right of every person to a consenting, loving relationship.

HOMOSEXUALITY AND THE OLD TESTAMENT

There is no specific Hebrew equivalent in the Hebrew Old Testament for the word *homosexuality* since the concept itself, as well as the English word origin, is nowhere found until the nineteenth century. Therefore the biblical teaching on homosexuality rests with the interpretations of the few passages that make references to persons of the same sex who engage in sexual intercourse. Our study will examine the interpretations of these passages by the pro-gay writers, and my responses to each of these interpretations.

The Holiness Code (Leviticus)

The major statement in the Old Testament about homosexuality is found in the book of Leviticus. Portions of the book, chapters 17–26, have been dubbed as the "Holiness Code" because of the repeated uses of the word *holy*. This code contains God's demands for ordering the life of His covenant people, Israel. This order has as its goal the setting apart of Israel from the immoral and idolatrous practices of her neighbors, so that she might be acceptable to worship the true and living God (cf. Leviticus 18:3). In this code are what appear to be two definite and direct prohibitions against homosexual acts.

> *Thou shalt not lie with a mankind as with womankind: it is an abomination.* (Leviticus 18:22)

> *And a man also lie with mankind as he lieth with a woman, both of them have committed an abomination: they shall surely be put to death; their blood shall be upon them.* (Leviticus 20:13)

This text stands amidst legislation against all impermissible and unnatural sexual relationships. Leviticus 20:13 restates 18:22, and adds the death penalty for the practice. Both call the homosexual act an *abomination* (*to'ebah,* in Hebrew). These commands expand the Seventh Commandment. Their purpose is not exhaustive regulation of sexual activity, but prohibition of the grossest of all sorts of offenses.

LGBT INTERPRETATION:

These two verses are often quoted to prove that homosexuality is *an abomination* to the Lord. However, it must be pointed out that the book of Leviticus was written to the nation Israel who was *under the Law.* We are the church and the apostle Paul clearly states over and over again that we are no longer under the law. *Christ redeemed us from the curse of the Law by becoming a curse for us* (Galatians 3:13). It was Jesus' death on the cross that rescued us from the curse of the law. If we insist on following the law and imposing the law on others, we negate the cross of Christ, and repudiate Christ's death on the cross (White, 2005*)*.

RESPONSE:

I cannot but agree with the point that Leviticus was addressed to Israel and Israel was under the Law and that we in the church age are no longer under the Law. Furthermore, I acknowledge that too often, we traditionalists have used this text to prove that homosexuality is an abomination to God in a way that suggests that it is a sin more grievous than others.

Nevertheless, we must not conclude that because we are no longer under the Law that it has no relevance for us in the church age. Let us first be reminded that *all Scripture is inspired by God and is profitable* (2 Timothy 3:16), even if it is not directly applicable to us. The apostle Paul reminds us that the experiences of God's people in the Old Testament are *"Now all of these things happened to them as examples and they were written for our admonition, on whom the end of the ages have come"* (1 Corinthians 10:11).

The Law reveals the character of God, and serves as a moral compass and God's prescription for holy conduct. The apostle tells us that *"we know the Law is good if one uses it lawfully* (1 Timothy 1:9). Every time homosexuality is mentioned in the Bible it is characterized as unholy, unlawful, and an abomination, whether it is singled out as in Leviticus 18:22; 20:13 or included in a list as in the New Testament (1 Corinthians 6:9-11; 1 Timothy 1:10-11).

PRO-GAY WRITERS offer a second understanding of the Holiness Code laws. They say homosexuality is condemned not because it is inherently wrong, but because it was practiced in the Old Testament world in connection with idolatrous, pagan rites. This view is expressed by almost every pro-homosexual writer.

Homosexuality, it is argued, is associated in the Jewish mind with idolatry, as can be seen in the passage such as Deuteronomy 23:17. This grows out of the fact that Israel's neighbors practiced fertility rites in their temple worship. God was understood as sexual, so worship included overt sexual acts. It is in this context that whenever homosexual acts are mentioned in the Old Testament, the writer has in mind the use that male worshipers made of male prostitutes.

Support for this position is found in the word *abomination (to'ebah),* which, on this view, does not signify something that is inherently evil such as rape or theft, but something that is ritually unclean, like the eating of pork or engaging in sexual intercourse during menstruation, both of which are prohibited in this context.

Temple prostitution is called an abomination and is condemned in 1 Kings 16:3, while prostitution in general is called "wickedness" *(zimmah)* and is prohibited in Leviticus 19:29. Sometimes the word *abomination* refers to an idol, as in Isaiah 44:19, Jeremiah 16:18, and Ezekiel 7:20. Specifically, it is claimed that Leviticus 18 has the purpose of distinguishing Israel from her pagan neighbors (18:3), and the prohibition of homosexuality follows directly after the condemnation of idolatrous sexuality (18:21). The same is true of chapter 20, which begins with the prohibition of sexual practice in connection with idolatry.

IN RESPONSE:

We must agree that, unquestionably, pagan religious rites included sexual activities, among which was male homosexuality. Participation in the idolatrous worship of the pagans was certainly forbidden and punished by God. His people Israel were not to be like their neighbors. However, that does not end the matter. Nothing in Leviticus explicitly states why the prohibited practices are condemned. The Leviticus texts just naturally assume the practices are condemned because they are inherently wrong, not because they are part of the idolatrous worship of the Egyptians and Canaanites.

In the Leviticus Code, incest, adultery, child sacrifice, bestiality, spiritism, and the cursing of one's parents are all prohibited. Only one act condemned in the code has cultic or symbolic significance—child sacrifice—and it is condemned whether associated with religious worship or not. Child sacrifice was practiced in pagan religious rites, but it was wrong on two counts—in itself and because of its association with idolatry. As a matter of fact, that the surrounding nations practiced both child sacrifice and the other prohibited acts only serves to confirm the corruption of these cultures in the mind of the Israelite.

Moreover, homosexuality is condemned in the context of adultery, bestiality, and incest. Clearly, these practices were not prohibited simply because of their association with idolatry or Egyptian and Canaanite cultures.

MOSAIC LAW—Another pro-gay handling of the Leviticus Holiness Code claims that the Mosaic Law or at least parts of it are irrelevant for the Christian today. In its most extreme form, this view argues that the Mosaic Law has *no* relevance for us today. All of it reflects folkways of an ancient culture. We live in the enlightened twenty-first century. Others say that since Christ is the end of the law for the Christian (Romans 10:4), even the Ten Commandments are no longer binding (2 Corinthians 3:7-11). The law has been superseded (Hebrews 7:11).

A weaker version of this position is used far more commonly. It distinguishes between the moral and ceremonial elements within the law. The former are still binding, but the latter have ended. Just as we need not feel obligated to follow the prohibitions in the law against eating rabbit (Leviticus 11:26), oysters, clams, shrimp, and lobster (Leviticus 11:10ff), or rare steaks (Leviticus 17:10), there is no need to adhere to prohibitions against homosexuality, since they, too, are a part of the ceremonial element of the law and so are not binding today.

IN RESPONSE:

This position in some forms contains an element of truth, but Old Testament law does not become irrelevant even for those holding a discontinuity position on the relation of the testaments. In fact, I believe that this is a classic example of a case where the Old Testament prohibition is clearly relevant, since the New Testament repeats the same command.

As to the matter of the ceremonial versus the moral elements of the law, we can again agree that there are differences. The problem is that the distinction is irrelevant to the question of homosexuality. While there are ceremonial elements in the law that we may safely disregard today, most Christians as well as Jews have always recognized that there are commands within the law that are of continuing ethical significance. Exodus 20–40 and Leviticus contain much of that material.

The Seed Is Sacred

Still, another approach used by pro-gay writers to these texts claims that the prohibitions against homosexuality are related to male dignity and the sacred character of the semen or "seed" of life.

They claim that the Hebrews, like other ancient peoples, had no accurate knowledge of the biology of conception. They did not know that women produce eggs which in turn are fertilized by male sperm. They thought that the seed for new life came solely from the man. It was "sowed" in a woman and grew into a new being in the same way that a plant sprouts and grows when sown in the ground.

Moreover, they did not know that mating between certain species would not produce offspring. Thus, men ought not to sow their seed where it would be unproductive (as would happen in homosexual relations) or in animals where it might result in "confusion," as in a centaur. This ignorance also explains why women are prohibited from receiving seed from an animal but are free to do among themselves what they please.

They further allege that in the patriarchal society of the Hebrews the position of the male was inviolable. It was not uncommon for the victors in war to rape conquered kings or soldiers as a mark of utter contempt and submission. In a male-dominated society, it is not unreasonable to think that homosexuality could be associated with effeminacy. At least one of the partners in male homosexual acts had to assume the position normally taken by a woman.

All of these things, then, would undermine the status and dignity of the male. *Therefore, it is not that homosexuality is morally wrong in itself, but that it is prohibited because of ignorance about conception and a desire to maintain the dominance of the male in a patriarchal society* (Rosner, 1981).

IN RESPONSE:

The Jewish attitude toward procreation is derived from the first commandment of God to Adam and Eve: ***"Be fruitful and multiply"*** (Genesis 1:28). There is nothing in the biblical text to support such an idea; therefore this view is purely speculative at best. Moreover, we cannot assume that the people of biblical times were as ignorant as supposed by the pro-gay writers (Schenker, 1987).

Finally, this argument totally ignores the inspiration of the Scriptures and the divine source of these commands. These commands are not the result of human speculation and superstition, but are from God and are found in the Bible. It is thus the conclusion of this writer that the Holiness Code is consistent with the other cited passages of the Old Testament in its condemnation of homosexuality as a sin.

Sodomy: Its Origin

From post-biblical times up to the present, the terms *sodomy* and *sodomite* have been used of homosexual practices in general. This usage has been based upon the interpretation of the narrative recorded in Genesis 19:1-25 in the city of Sodom. The narrative records the incident when two men (angels) came into the city of Sodom, and Lot, as was the custom, extended hospitality to them by offering them food and lodging for the night. After the two men had dined,

"the men of the city, the men of Sodom, both old and young all the people from every quarter, surrounded the house. And they called to Lot and said to him, 'Where are the men who came to you tonight? Bring them down to us that we may know them carnally . . . for we will destroy this place because the outcry against them has grown great before the face of the Lord, and the Lord has sent us to destroy it' . . . then the Lord rained brimstone and fire on Sodom and Gomorrah from the Lord out of the heavens" (Genesis 19:4, 5, 13, 24, NKJV)

THE TRADITIONAL INTERPRETATION of this passage is that the angels were sent to Sodom and Gomorrah to confirm their wickedness which had risen as an outcry to the Lord. Proof of the level of their wickedness is seen in the demand of the men of the city to Lot, to bring the male angels out to them for the purpose of *"knowing them carnally,"* which is interpreted as their desiring them to have sex with them.

In confirmation of sodomy as a sin, a wickedness of high degree, the Lord destroyed the cities of Sodom and Gomorrah by raining down fire and brimstone from heaven. *The terms* sodomy *and* sodomite *arise out of the actions of the sodomites, the men of the city of Sodom.*

THE LGBT INTERPRETATION of this passage challenges the traditional interpretation in at least two ways. First, some have argued that if the sin of Sodom and Gomorrah was sexual, it was not simply homosexual but *homosexual rape.* Lot's plea to the men of the town, they allege, was not to *rape* the visitors. They go on to say that to use this passage to condemn homosexuality because of homosexual rape is no more justified that condemning heterosexuality because of instances of heterosexual rape. The sinfulness of any rape lies not in the fact that it is homosexual or heterosexual in character, but in the fact that it victimizes a non-consenting partner (Religious Tolerance.org, Anthony Ashford).

IN RESPONSE:
I agree that the men of Sodom desired to rape the angelic visitors, but I disagree with the interpretation that the sin focused upon *consent* rather than

the act itself. Nowhere does the text even slightly hint that what the men wanted to do would be permissible if only Lot's guests had consented. Moreover, this interpretation does not account for the fact that God's judgment fell upon the entire city. Was homosexual rape a common practice and thus brought the judgment of God? It could have been, but such is not stated in the text.

What is more damaging to this interpretation is that God's judgment on homosexuality in Sodom and Gomorrah is quite in harmony with this prohibition and denunciation of this in other Scriptures that are properly interpreted. One of the rules of hermeneutics is "Scripture interprets Scripture." It is not as though this is the only time homosexuality is denounced and judged (Romans 1:26-27; 2 Peter 2:6; Jude 7).

LGBT: A VIOLATION OF THE HOSPITALITY CODE—A second pro-gay interpretation of Genesis 19 is even bolder, for it claims the passage is not about homosexuality at all. Rather, the sin of Sodom and Gomorrah related to a gross violation of the hospitality code.

"Hospitality to strangers was a virtue exemplified by Abraham (Genesis 18:1-8) and Lot (Genesis 19:1-3) and an important virtue expected of noble-minded people. Contrarily, the oppression of the stranger as exemplified by (the attempted gang rape at Lot's house) in Genesis 19:1-9 was, according to ancient Semitic custom, a very grave crime" (Brownlee, 1986).

Sodom and Gomorrah were exceedingly wicked cities. God determined to find out the truth about their reputation, so He sent two angels to investigate. They came to the city one evening and were met at the gate by Lot, who invited them to his home for hospitality. Before the visitors retired for the night, the inhabitants of the city demanded to meet and get acquainted with the visitors.

This demand to meet the angelic visitors grew out of Lot's serious breach of hospitality rules. Lot was a resident alien, a sojourner. In return for the protection and toleration of the city, he had certain obligations, some of which pertained to visitors. This incident arose in regard to those obligations.

Lot, either ignorantly or intentionally, exceeded the rights of an alien resident in receiving and entertaining two "foreigners." The visitors might have hostile intentions, so it was not unreasonable to require that their credentials be examined. The visitors should have been received first by the Sodomites. Moreover, the men of Sodom's suspicions of these visitors may have been heightened because Lot does not seem to have been a man of pleasing character, for Genesis says that though he was a sojourner, he acted as a judge among them.

This interpretation is supported by three lines of argument. First, the Hebrew word *yada'* is found 943 times in the Old Testament. It is used only ten times without qualification (excluding this text and its derivative, Judges 19:22) to refer to sexual relations, and always of heterosexual relations. Had homosexual relations been in view, then the Hebrew word *shakab* would be expected. *Shakab* is used some fifty times in the Old Testament for sexual intercourse, relations between men and women, men and men, and even humans and animals. Thus, *yada'* must be taken in its common meaning of "to know" or "to get acquainted with." The men of Sodom and Gomorrah were simply interested in getting to know the angelic visitors.

The hospitality breach interpretation is also supported by the way other biblical texts refer to Sodom and Gomorrah. That is, it is argued, the interpretation of Sodom's sin as homosexuality is not supported by intra-biblical exegesis.

Examine Isaiah 1:9; Jeremiah 23:14; Ezekiel 16:48, 49; Matthew 10:14-15; and Luke 10:10-12. These passages use Sodom and Gomorrah as symbols of utter destruction, and their sin is said to be so great that it deserves exemplary punishment. These passages, however, make no mention of sexual sin. They either mention the arrogance of the cities or their lack of hospitality.

IN RESPONSE TO THE "HOSPITALITY BREACH" INTERPRETATION:

I agree that the hospitality code was an important custom and to violate it might be seen as a serious crime. However, I am not at all convinced that this is the case here for several reasons.

First, it should be noted that though the word *yada'* may be used as simply "to know" or "get acquainted with," it may also be used to denote something other than what is claimed by the pro-gay writers. Five times in the book of Genesis we find the word *yada'* used to denote sexual relationships.

"And Adam knew (yada) Eve his wife, and she conceived and bare Cain" (Genesis 4:1, KJV). *"And Cain knew (yada) his wife and she conceived, and bare Enoch"* (Genesis 4:17). See also Genesis 24:16; 25; 38:26.

Moreover, it is used in this passage to refer to Lot's offer of his daughters, *"Behold I have two daughters who have not known (yada) man"* (19:8). It is clear that he is offering them for their sexual pleasure, for surely they were already acquainted with men in the city. It is very unlikely that the same verb in a single narrative should have two different meanings without some indication in the text, particularly when the uses of the verb occur so close together.

It should also be noted that contrary to what is claimed above, the Hebrew word *shakab* may be used with sexual connotations or simply to lying down for sleep: *"Before they lay down (shakab) the men of the city"* (19:4).

An examination of the Pentateuch reveals that Moses uses the term more than fifty times to refer to sexual relationships, providing overwhelming evidence that his usage of the word here must be taken to mean that the men of the city wanted to know the visitors sexually. A clear parallel use of the verb *yada'* is seen in the story of the old man in Judges 19:22. *"Bring forth the man that came into thine house, that we may know (yada) him . . . so the man took his concubine, and brought her forth unto them; and they knew (yada) her"* (Judges 19:16-27).

Finally, if all the men of Sodom wanted was to investigate the visitors' credentials, Lot's offer of his daughters for sexual pleasure makes no sense. Why did Lot not just introduce his guests and demonstrate their good intentions?

It is helpful here to remind ourselves of the principle of interpretation that says, "If the common sense makes sense, seek no other sense." The common sense of the use of the verb *yada'* here is sexual. Therefore, we must reject the violation of the hospitality code interpretation of this text.

As to the way other Scriptures refer to Sodom and Gomorrah, it is true that not every reference to them condemns their sexual sins. But neither do those texts exclude homosexuality as at least part of the cause of divine judgment. The two cities were exceedingly wicked, and their utter destruction is graphic evidence of that. Even those who defend a non-sexual interpretation of the text recognize that Sodom was so wicked that she was destroyed for many reasons. Furthermore, the sins mentioned in the texts cited are quite in keeping with the kinds of sins Romans 1 describes, of which sexual sins are only a part.

Jude gives a striking commentary on the sin of Sodom. It is called *"going after strange or different flesh"* (*sarkasheteras*), which is a way of describing unnatural sex acts. Jude uses the verb *porneuo* with the preposition *ek,* which means they gave themselves up to sexual immorality completely and utterly. This is an extremely strong statement. These kinds of sins make the complete destruction of the two cities understandable. While we realize that arrogance and inhospitality are terrible sins, they cannot explain the judgment of the destruction of two entire cities.

Finally, we must reject the breach of hospitality interpretation because it seems unjust. If the problem at Sodom was that the hospitality code was broken, it was Lot who broke it, not the inhabitants of Sodom. So it was Lot who should have been judged, but, instead, Lot and his family were the only ones who escaped while Sodom and Gomorrah were destroyed. Such injustice cannot come from a holy and just God.

For all these reasons, this author finds these LGBT interpretations of Genesis 19 unacceptable. They simply do not square with sound hermeneutics or with the whole counsel of Scripture that condemn homosexuality as a sin.

David and Jonathan: Homosexual Relationship?

Before leaving the Old Testament, allow me to simply acknowledge and summarily dismiss the claims of some pro-gay writers who suggest that the relationship between David and Jonathan was homosexual.

This claim like those previously examined seeks to use the Hebrew language to validate their position. And like those above, it is guilty of selecting Scriptures that support their claim while ignoring those which do not. This claim focuses upon the Hebrew word *ahab*, "to have affection for, sexually or otherwise" (*Hebrew Greek Key Study Bible #157*).

It is used to describe Jonathan and David's affection for one another in several passages: *"Jonathan was knit to the soul of David, and Jonathan loved (ahab) him as his own soul"* (1 Samuel 18:1, NKJV). *"Then Jonathan and David made a covenant, because he loved (ahab) him as his own soul"* (1 Samuel 18:3, NKJV). *"I am distressed for you, my brother Jonathan; you have been very pleasant to me; your love (ahab) to me was wonderful, surpassing the love (ahab) of women"* (2 Samuel 1:26, NKJV). According to one pro-gay writer this story demonstrates that "two people of the same sex may live in a loving, committed relationship with God's favor" *(GayChristian.net)*.

This claim must be rejected because it ignores the fact that the Hebrew word *ahab* is used in the Old Testament in other passages that clearly do not refer to anything sexual. For example, it is used of Abraham in describing his affection for Isaac, *"And he said, Take thy son, thine only son, whom thou lovest (ahab)"* (Genesis 22:2, KJV). The best-known usage of the word is in the Decalogue where we are commanded, *"Thou shall love (ahab) thy neighbor as thyself"* (Leviticus 19:18; Exodus 20:4-6). These usages clearly have no sexual connotation.

It is more likely that David's comparison of his relationship with Jonathan as surpassing those with women is probably a reference to his experience with King Saul's daughter whom he was promised for killing Goliath. The king, however, continued to renege on his promise by adding conditions and stipulations. David is most likely saying that the love he received from Jonathan was greater than anything he could have received from Saul's daughter.

Conclusion

In concluding this study on homosexuality in the Old Testament, it is instructional to note that the morality of the Old Testament remains the same today as is reaffirmed by the Rabbinical Council of America (RCA), the nation's largest body of Orthodox Jews, "The Torah and Jewish tradition, in the clearest of terms, prohibit the practice of homosexuality" (J. Lee Grady, *Charisma,* June 2013).

We, like the priests in David's day, must acknowledge that the Old Testament cannot in letter or spirit be used to prove the claim that God approves of homosexuality.

HOMOSEXUALITY AND THE NEW TESTAMENT
Romans 1:26-27

For this cause God gave them up unto vile affections: for even their women did change the natural use into that which is against nature: and likewise also the men, leaving the natural use of the woman, burned in their lust one toward another; men with men working that which is unseemly, and receiving in themselves that recompence of their error which was meet. (Romans 1:26-27, KJV)

This text is by far the most popularly referenced text cited by those who claim that homosexuality is condemned, as it seems to be the strongest condemnation of such actions. Verse 26 deals with lesbianism while verse 27 treats male homosexuality. This, by the way, is the only text in Scripture that mentions female homosexuality. The traditional interpretation of this passage is that it teaches that homosexual practices are evidences of God's judgment on those who reject his revelation.

LGBT: THE ABUSE ARGUMENT—By far, the most common pro-gay interpretation of this passage is that called "The Abuse Argument." The argument goes like this: What Paul is condemning is *unnatural, abusive* homosexual actions. That is to say, that he is not condemning homosexuality in general, only a certain kind of homosexual *act*.

In support of this the pro-gay proponents use the illustration of eating and gluttony. The Bible, they point out, does not condemn eating, but it does condemn gluttony, which is an abuse of eating. Likewise they reason that God does not condemn homosexual intercourse, but He does condemn the abuse of such intercourse. God does not condemn loving, consensual sex between two males who are living in a committed, non-abusive relationship (Boswell, 1980).

LGBT: INVERTS NOT PERVERTS—Pro-gay writers point out that this text demands an understanding of the difference between *inverts* and *perverts;* the former are *natural* and the latter are *unnatural*.

Perverts are not genuinely homosexual. They engage in homosexual practices, although they are heterosexuals. Some in this group may be referred to as those on the "DL" (down-low) referenced earlier.

Inverts, on the other hand, are *constitutionally* gay. They prefer members of the same sex and experience no attraction to members of the opposite sex. Their sexual orientation is the *inverse* of heterosexuals, and for them, engaging in homosexual acts is normal. In the passage above, Romans 1:26-27, the apostle Paul *condemns perversion, not inversion.*

Support for this view is adduced from Paul's claim that those he discusses changed or left the *natural* use of their sexuality for that which was *unnatural* or against nature. Thus, Paul only condemns homosexual acts committed by apparently heterosexual persons. This, so it is claimed, is in keeping with the point of Romans 1, which has as its purpose the stigmatization of those who reject their calling.

For those who reject this view and appeal to Paul's claim that homosexuality goes "against nature," their response is that "against nature" is difficult to interpret, but it must mean a variation from what is usual or normal. The homosexual is not desirous that everyone should be like him or her in sexual preference. *Homosexuality is a variation from the normal (i.e., heterosexual).*

It is not, they argue, a sin or disorder. Nature is full of variations from its overall design. Some people are midgets, others are albinos, still others are left-handed. These, like homosexuals, are and always will be minority variations from the majority. These differences are not unique to our culture and time. They have always existed and will continue to do so. They evidence neither sin nor the fallen condition of humanity, but merely the lack of uniformity in nature. Rather than condemn them, they argue, we should affirm them and rejoice that they exist.

IN RESPONSE:

Despite these claims, careful exegesis of the text does not support this view. First, it must be pointed out that this interpretation requires one to accept as true what is yet to be determined, namely, that there is a constitutional homosexual for whom homosexual acts follow from a genetic condition. As has been pointed out in the conclusion of the scientific studies above, it has not yet been proved that a person can be born gay. Moreover, there is no evidence to believe that if such a condition exists that Paul knew of it and refers to it here.

Furthermore, it is most unlikely that when Paul says they gave up the natural use of their sexuality and did that which was against nature *(para phusin)* he is referring to homosexual acts by heterosexuals, acts that would be against their natural inclinations. This is the most reasonable thought.

Nor is it likely that Paul asserts, as others claim, that some people are just different from the norm, but there is no penalty for such variation. Instead, these verses teach that homosexual acts are against the order of sexuality established in nature (an order clearly revealed in Genesis 1 and 2) and is evidence that God has judicially given over those who practice these acts to their own lusts.

As to the claim that homosexuality is merely a variation from the norm as are midgets, albinos, etc., it must again be pointed out that this view requires proof that such a variation exists constitutionally. Moreover, none of these variations are identified or equated with sin or idolatry as is homosexuality.

IDOLATRY CONDEMNED, NOT HOMOSEXUALITY—The LGBT says this text does not condemn homosexuality *per se*, but only such acts in connection with idolatry. "The center of Paul's argument in this text is not homosexuality but idolatry"

(Peter J. Gomes, Duke University Chapel speaker). Gomes goes on to say that the "degrading passions refer to the worship of sexual pleasure, an excess to be condemned with all other excesses."

The use of homosexuality by Paul in this text is simply to illustrate his main point which is that no one is without excuse when it comes to sin, *There is no one who is righteous, not even one* (Romans 3:23). Gomes goes on to point out that the only forms of homosexuality Paul could have had in mind when he wrote these verses were exploitive forms of homosexuality, such as Greek pederasty, Roman prostitution, and/or temple prostitutes of Canaanite fertility religions which were both male and female. "The idea of a committed same-sex relationship would have never entered Paul's mind. Therefore, it is quite a stretch to use these verses to condemn monogamous committed same-sex relationships in the 21st century" ("I'm Christian, I'm Gay, Let's Talk," Pastor David Eck, Evangelical Lutheran Church, Asheville, NC).

These verses are found in the context of condemning idolatry, superstition, and other ungodly beliefs and in no way should be seen as a condemnation of homosexuality.

IN RESPONSE:

Much of what has already been said about the connection of homosexual practice with idolatry applies here and needs not to be repeated. However, I do think it is worth noting here as above, the primary argument of the pro-gay writers focus on the phrase **"against *nature*,"** which, according to gay writer Boswell, always involves possession, which means if a thing is against someone's nature, then it is a thing he or she would not normally do.

A much better interpretation of the text, however, will show that the apostle is referring to creation and the natural order of things as God created them. In creation God created them, man and woman, and the natural order is heterosexuality. The apostle, here, cites homosexuality as going **"against nature,"** contrary to the natural order and His intentions for men and women. The idea is that the apostle's writings should be seen against the background of the culture of the Jews and the non-believing Greeks and thus restricted in its application to that period of time. I need to point out that in establishing heterosexuality as the natural order for procreation and reproduction, men have genitals and females have vaginas in all cultures and for all times. Homosexuality is against nature because homosexuals cannot reproduce.

LGBT: WRONG MOTIVE, NOT HOMOSEXUALITY CONDEMNED—A third main line of interpretation of this passage claims that it does not condemn homosexuality *per se,* but only homosexual acts growing out of lust, which is a wrong motive.

Paul's comment in 1:27 *that they burned in their lust for one another* is the key to understanding what he condemns. Lust is wrong. Any activity produced by lust is immoral, whether it is homosexual or heterosexual. The only moral sexual activity is that which grows out of love and devotion. *Therefore, if homosexual acts are motivated by a sense of love, devotion, and commitment, they are part of God's design for human sexuality.*

IN RESPONSE:

The problem with this interpretation is that the text does not say that *because* of homosexual acts, God has given them over to this lust for one another. *The lustful desire is a consequence of their sinful homosexual acts.*

LGBT: FALSE RIGHTEOUSNESS CONDEMNED, NOT HOMOSEXUALITY is a final approach to Romans 1:26-27. Hence, Paul's mention of homosexuality in Romans 1 is quite incidental to the real object of his attack—false religion (Romans 2). His real concern is those Jews who thought they were keeping the law and were thereby righteous. In Romans 1 he simply adopts a common catalog of vices from extra-biblical sources without endorsing its judgments in order to portray the sins of the Gentiles. But this list is incidental to his main attack on the religious complacency of Pharisaism.

IN RESPONSE:

On the contrary, this interpretation overlooks the fact that the argument of Romans 1 and 2 leads to a ringing condemnation of both Gentiles and Jews in chapter 3 that takes quite seriously the sins of both. Moreover, if Paul's actual attack is on Jewish self-righteousness, Romans 1 adds nothing to that topic. What function does it serve in the epistle?

Conclusion

The analysis of the alternate interpretations presented above has led this writer to conclude that the traditional understanding of Romans 1:26-27 is correct: *homosexuality is condemned.* Paul states very clearly that homosexuality is God's judgment that punishes those who reject the truth of God's revelation about Himself. Homosexuality is among the idolatrous activities prohibited by God. Idolatrous behavior is invariably self-destructive as God gives up idolaters to the consequences of their rebellion. In essence it is the result of man's freely made choice to reject God.

1 Corinthians 6:9-11 and 1 Timothy 1:8-10

Do you not know that the unrighteous will not inherit the kingdom? Do not be deceived. Neither fornicators, nor idolaters, nor adulterers, nor homosexuals, nor sodomites, nor thieves, nor covetous, nor drunkards, nor revilers, nor extortioners will inherit the kingdom of God. And such were some of you. But you were washed, but you were sanctified, but you were justified in the name of the Lord Jesus and by the Spirit of our God.
(1 Corinthians 6:9-11, NKJV)

But we know that the law is good if one uses it lawfully, knowing this: that the law is not made for a righteous person, but for the lawless and insubordinate, for the ungodly and for sinners, for the unholy and profane, for murderers of fathers and murderers of mothers, for manslayers, for fornicators, for sodomites, for kidnappers, for liars, for perjurers, and if there is any other thing that is contrary to sound doctrine. (1 Timothy 1:8-10, NKJV)

As an illustration of how translators give interpretations reflecting their biases, see below the translation of these verses in *The Message,* a LGBT-friendly publication:

Don't you realize that this is not the way to live? Unjust people who don't care about God will not be joining in his kingdom. Those who use and abuse each other, use and abuse sex, use and abuse the earth and everything in it, don't qualify as citizens in God's kingdom. A number of you know from experience what I am talking about, for not so long ago you were on that list. Since then, you've been cleaned up and given a fresh start by Jesus, our Master, our Messiah, and by our God present in us, the Spirit. (1 Corinthians 6:9-11, *The Message*; cited by Pastor David Eck, July 15, 2011)

These two passages from Paul will complete our study of the major biblical texts in the New Testament on this subject. I am grouping 1 Corinthians 6:9-11 and 1 Timothy 1:8-10 together because they both contain vice lists which include a similar word that bears on our discussion.

In 1 Corinthians 6:9-11 Paul talks about those who will not inherit the kingdom of God. He gives a list of vices and says that anyone who persists in these sins will not inherit the kingdom of God. In 1 Timothy 1:8-10 the law is the subject, and Paul says it is good if used wisely. It is not for the righteous man, but for the ungodly and sinners. He then describes in a vice list sins that the ungodly and sinners commit.

In the 1 Corinthians passage Paul includes in his list the Greek words *malakoi* and *arsenokoitai*. The 1 Timothy list also includes *arsenokoitai*. These Greek words have been translated variously in English versions of the Bible. The King James Version renders them *"effeminate"* and *"abusers of themselves with mankind."*

The New American Standard Bible retains *"effeminate"* but prefers *"homosexual"* for the second word, while the New International Version uses *"male prostitute"* and *"homosexual offender."* As we shall see, there is some uncertainty about the precise meaning of these Greek terms. But the majority opinion has been that the first term refers to the passive partner in a homosexual relationship and the second to the active member.

LGBT: VICE LISTS ONLY—The first response to these verses by pro-homosexual interpreters is that these actions are not singled out in these lists as being especially wicked, and if we were to take vice lists seriously, no one would enter into the kingdom of God, since we are all guilty of at least one of these sins. Lists of this sort was common in Greco-Roman literature and was labeled by scholars as a "catalog of vices." It consists of a list of evil habits and attitudes with no apparent rhyme or reason for their selection or order.

"The list was a club used to hit an opponent over the head or to warn the writer's own community of the penalty for evil living" (Eck). The lists were apparently traditional and its importance was not to identify any particular sin but to simply impress the reader of the activities disapproved by God. "Any relation between an individual item in a list and the situation addressed was thus, more often than not, nonexistent. . . . It is clear that the apostle does not care about any specific item in the lists" (Eck).

The correct interpretation of this list focuses upon a correct understanding of the Greek words *malakoi* and *arsenokoitai*. The first term, *malakoi*, literally means "soft" or "males who are soft." This word has been translated as "effeminate" (KJV), "homosexuals" (NKJV), and "male prostitutes" (NIV, NRSV). Only in the twentieth century has it been understood to be a reference to homosexuality. It commonly designated any male whose behavior was less than respectable. Many scholars argue that *malakoi* refers to moral weakness in general.

The second term, *arsenokoitai*, is an uncommon word and its meaning is equally ambiguous as is indicated by the variations in translations: "abusers of themselves with mankind" (KJV); "sexual perverts" (RSV); "sodomites" (NKJV, NRSV); "those who are guilty of homosexual perversion" (NEB); "homosexual offenders" (NIV). Pro-gay writer John Boswell says that it was not until the fourth century that the term referred to anything other than male prostitutes and would have been the way the apostle used it here. As such, what is here being condemned is male prostitution and not homosexuality per se.

IN RESPONSE:

As has already been pointed out in our study of the subject in the Old Testament, to say that a sin in a long list does not draw special condemnation does not mean Scripture approves the action. A vice list is still a vice list.

In evaluating this position, it is only fair to note that there is some difference of opinion about the meaning of these terms, but their meaning is not nearly as unclear as pro-homosexual writers want us to believe. In classical Greek, *malakos* is used of boys and men who allow themselves to be used homosexually, and of those who play the part of the passive partner in homosexual intercourse. In "Roman Antiquities," written about 7 BC by Dionysius of Halicarnassus, Aristodemus of Cumae is called *malakos* because he had been "effeminate" (the ludrias) as a child, having undergone things associated with women.

Thus, while there is some ambiguity about *malakos*, there is evidence in supporting the view that it refers to the passive partner in homosexual intercourse. Moreover, this view is further supported by its use with *arsenokoites*, a term for the active member in such acts. Aristotle in "Problems" has a lengthy discussion on the origins of homosexual passivity, and he uses the word *malakos*.

The second of these terms, *arsenokoites,* is used by Paul in both 1 Corinthians 6:9 and 1 Timothy 1:10. Pro-gay writer Boswell claims that it has only tangential relationship to homosexuality. His point seems to be that it is found in a list of sexual sins, sexual immorality *(pornos)*, adultery (which is referred to in the passage by referring to adulterers *(moichoi)*, and effeminacy *(malakos)*. However, rather than strengthening Boswell's position, his point seems to weaken it. *Arsenokoites* is related to sexual sin; it is among sexual sins in Paul's list.

Further, Boswell's case is weakened by the fact that both *malakos* and *arsenokoites* follow *pornos* in Paul's vice lists. *Pornos* is a general term for sexual sin and is often, as in the texts under consideration, followed by specific examples.

Conclusion

In concluding our study on the biblical teaching on homosexuality, allow me again to acknowledge that there are a surprisingly small number of texts that speak directly to homosexuality. However, after carefully examining each of the texts that address the subject—from Creation to the Holiness Codes in the book of Leviticus, to the Mosaic Law and to the teachings of the apostle Paul in the New Testament—*we cannot escape the clear conviction that when Scripture does speak of homosexuality, it prohibits and condemns it and therefore it must be prohibited and condemned by the church.*

CHAPTER

7

Homosexuality and Homophobia in the Black Church

Is the black church homophobic? Although the answer to the question may seem obvious, we must take care to note the fact that when people use the term, they do not always do so with the same meaning in mind. Sometimes a person will even switch from one definition to another in the middle of a conversation or debate without making a distinction.

In discussing this issue with my brethren across the country who serve in the pastorate, I have come to the conclusion that the overwhelming majority of them see themselves as loving the homosexual but hating the homosexual behavior—although I must acknowledge that more than a few find even the suggestion of homosexual orientation detestable.

Most of them are conservatives who believe in the inspiration and inerrancy of Scripture and interpret the Bible literally. For them, they see the half dozen or so Scriptures, which we have examined previously, as condemning all homosexual behavior. They feel that their beliefs and practices are biblically based and, in accordance with their responsibility as pastors and overseers of the flock, homosexuality is something they must oppose.

They deeply resent being characterized as "homophobes" for simply carrying out what they believe to be the Word of God.

Of course we would do well to remember that, in the same way, Southern Baptists, and many others during the nineteenth century, resented being condemned for what they considered their moral, biblical stand in favor of slavery. Also, many evangelical Christians in the South supported segregation on biblical grounds as late as the middle of the twentieth century, but objected to being called racists.

WHAT DOES IT MEAN TO BE HOMOPHOBIC?

Like the terms *gay* and *homosexual*, the term *homophobic* is even more difficult. What determines whether or not one is homophobic? In seeking an answer to this question, it is needful first to examine the many ways in which the term *homophobia* is used in our society. The word *homophobia* was invented by George Weinbert, who defined it as *"the dread of being in close quarters with homosexuals."* It grew to mean a general *"fear of homosexuals or of homosexual behavior."* Homophobia, like a number of related words, can be shown to have dual meanings—one related to feelings and another related to actions. For example, a person who believes women are intrinsically inferior to men (or vice versa) is sometimes referred to as a sexist—a person who exhibits sexism. Other times, the same word is used to refer to an action: a person who discriminates against women (or men) as a group. One can only infer which definition is in use within a given communication act from the context in which the word is used.

This single word, *homophobic*, is hopelessly inadequate to cover the full range of people's negative beliefs and actions about individuals of minority sexual orientations and sexual behaviors. Different meanings assigned to this word are as follows:

Meanings based on actions: This refers to those who actively work toward defining homosexuals in such a way that they are to be denied certain rights normally granted heterosexuals, such as the right to marry.

Meanings based on belief and feelings: This may refer to individuals who hate or dislike persons with a homosexual orientation. Or, it may refer to individuals who attempt to love the homosexual while condemning homosexual activity as a sin hated by God. It may also refer to those who disagree with but are afraid to speak out against it.

When applied to the black church, and as used in the title of this book, *homophobia* may be defined as "the fear or uneasiness of being in close proximity to homosexuals and homosexual behavior, including being fearful to publicly condemn it as a sin."

With that as my working definition, the black church must undeniably be considered homophobic.

THE LAW OF NON-CONTRADICTION

The law of non-contradiction states that two opposite statements cannot both be true. Second, the law of non-contradiction cannot be denied without being affirmed—it is literally undeniable. The very affirmation that "Opposites can both be true" (a denial of the law) implies that the opposite is not true. One cannot make a meaningful statement about anything that does not entail the affirmation that the statement's opposite is false (which is what is meant by the law of non-contradiction).

In my lectures and discussions on the subject of homosexuality and its causes with our people from across the country, I oftentimes pose two questions. First, I ask them, "By a show of hands, how many of you believe that a person cannot be born gay?" In response, the overwhelming number raise their hands in agreement. I then ask, "How many of you knew of someone in your family or in your neighborhood who behaved gay or homosexual at an early age and everyone agreed that the child was born like that?" Again, the overwhelming number of those present raise their hands, indicating that they had indeed known of someone whom everyone in the community agreed was born a "sissy."

The law of non-contradiction says that both cannot be true. We cannot on the one hand affirm that a person cannot be born gay, and on the other hand affirm that we knew someone whom everyone agreed was born gay.

At the suggestion of my pastor, Dr. Joe B. Maddox, I decided to statistically test this thesis with a brief survey at several churches and a district association where I have lectured over the past thirty years as a teaching evangelist. The survey and the results are in the Appendix of this book.

ANECDOTAL TESTIMONIES: "BUSTER" AND "JABO"

Unless we are willing to discount *all* of the testimonies of *all* of us who affirm that we knew someone who was born gay, along with *all* of the testimonies of those who claim to have been born gay, then we must be willing to at least *entertain* the possibility of such. The fact that we cannot understand and the sciences cannot explain how a person can be born gay must not make us deny the reality of the existence of individuals who are *apparently* constitutionally gay. I use the term *apparently* because there is no other explanation for what we see before us in living color. The first step in confronting homophobia must begin with this acknowledgment.

I recognize how difficult such an acknowledgment will be for those of us who have maintained that such cannot be. So allow me here to recite a story told to me by a close acquaintance, because it is a story that is representative of scores of such stories told by many others. It is the story of his older brother, whom for the sake of privacy we shall call "Buster."

My friend said, "Buster was my older brother, and he never discussed with me the subject of homosexuality. But from my earliest recollection of him, it was apparent that he was not like most of us boys. First, he was different in his intelligence. I can earnestly say that even as a child, the signs of genius were evident as he astonished one and all with his brilliance.

He continued, "We didn't know anything about homosexuality back in those days, deep in the rural southern part of Alabama in the late 1940s. On the outskirts of Selma, where we were born and reared, our community was closed to outside influences to sway us in our sexual orientation one way or the other. So closed was our community that we were not allowed to even speak with other children outside of church, school, and family functions. We did, however, know of the word *sissy*, and that simply meant that a boy had the mannerisms of a girl, how they switched when they walked and their apparent 'high strung' nature."

He told me that there was no male or father figure in their family. His mother raised the seven of them alone. "My brother Buster, as the oldest and the most willing, performed all of the duties normally relegated to females. Like a duck taking to the water. All of these duties—cooking, cleaning, diapering, washing, and bathing—seemed to come so natural to him. He even had the authority to discipline us as it seemed best to him, something I resented immensely, as he was only two years my elder."

My buddy said that he was always convinced that Buster had become "sissified" because he was forced to take on the role of a female. He said, "My mother had four boys from another marriage; so when my father abandoned us, Buster had to take care of all six of us. I remember distinctly how deeply I resented the ease with which Buster accepted all of these feminine duties, especially that of disciplining me."

He recalled how he had a conversation with his Aunt Dorothy, who was only seven years older than him, and how he shared with her his conclusions about why Buster acted the way he did. He said that his aunt interrupted him to make the case that "Buster acted like a girl as early as age three or four!" She recounted that when their mother would drop them off at her house, while she went off to work, his brother Buster would literally tear off his pants and shirt and find one of her dresses and re-dress himself.

His aunt said that Buster, after dressing up like a girl, would proclaim loudly, "I am not a boy; I am just as much a girl as you are!" She reminded him that as early as then, Buster did not enjoy playing the games that the other boys in the neighborhood played. He remembered seeing Buster through the window and how they made fun of him for being such a sissy, for playing with dolls, and for prancing around in high-heel shoes like a woman.

He said, "My mother never addressed the issue, but my Aunt Mildred would become embarrassed, cringing with every move Buster made like a girl." He and his other brothers especially hated Buster's behavior, because he had the body of a pure-bred athlete. At the age of twelve, he was six feet tall and weighed two hundred pounds. "Of course that meant that he could physically whip any and all of us, individually or collectively. So no matter how he chose to dress or act, we left him alone!"

My friend said that his aunt and everyone in the neighborhood agreed that "Buster was born that way!" Moreover, all efforts to change him were met with resentment by him. The doctors were baffled because, in spite of the fact that his IQ exceeded 150, they were not able to get through to him. "Buster didn't want to be fixed! He knew who he was and how he was, and he did not try to hide it. So we all accepted it and no one tried to confront or change him."

He said that Buster moved away from home while still a teenager and tried to date women for a while, but found it unfulfilling. By the time he reached age fifteen, he became withdrawn and suicidal. He ended up being incarcerated, and still is today. He became a full-blown practicing homosexual. Whenever he is mentioned in family conversations, we all agree: "He was born gay!"

As the survey indicated, many of us have had a "Buster" in our lives. Mine was named Jabo (not his real name).

JABO, MY CHILDHOOD FRIEND

I was born in Birmingham, Alabama, in 1942, and I lived there with my maternal grandparents. Our community was near downtown and included the historical Sixteenth Street Baptist Church, remembered for the 1963 bombing by the KKK that killed three little girls. Our community was the inner city of the 1940s; and in many ways it was not unlike the inner cities of today, with the exception that it was more closed because of Jim Crow laws of segregation.

Of course everyone knew everyone else—who their folks were, who lived with whom, who was fatherless, who was shacking, who was pimping, who was bootlegging liquor, and so forth. Although we lived within ear-shot of downtown Birmingham and eyesight of city hall, our immediate neighborhood had no park or playground. Consequently, we worked together as a community and annually cleared the nearby field that served as our playground, putting up a basketball goal in the spring, and lining it off for baseball in the summer and football in the winter.

Before each game played, we chose sides. The boys who had over time—through previous games and more than a few fights—proved themselves to be the best athletes (the strongest, the fastest, and most of all, the toughest) were given the honor of choosing who would be on whose team.

In every instance, the first one doing the choosing, the one whom everyone agreed was the toughest kid in the 'hood, was a boy called "Jabo." The thing that was perplexing about Jabo, though, was the fact that he was a "sissy." He acted like a girl in his mannerisms, flipping his wrists when he talked and switching his rear like a girl when he walked.

Of course, with Jabo's prowess, no one dared to mess with him; so bullying him was not even a thought. As a matter of fact, among the worst-kept secrets was that Jabo, who was a couple of years older than me, would invite boys entering puberty to meet him at some spot later on. This became such a practice that an invitation from Jabo was akin to a "rite of passage" for boys in our 'hood. For some, Jabo may have been their first sexual experience.

Everyone in the neighborhood accepted as factual that Jabo was "born gay" because as early as anyone could remember he always acted like a girl. There was not, however, any homophobia as such about Jabo; he was accepted along with everyone else. In the neighborhood, we had some guys who were drunks, some who were punks, some who were hustlers, some who were preachers, some who were gamblers, and a few who were sissies.

I left Birmingham when I turned twelve. Perhaps because I was a skinny kid, I never received an invite from Jabo. However, in recent conversations with my brother in Chicago (who keeps in touch with everyone back home) and my uncle, who still lives there, I am told that Jabo died just a few years ago. His funeral was widely attended, and many who did so testified of his character as a good person, with no references to his sexuality.

The point that I am trying to make here in these narratives is that *homosexuality has always been a part of the black community. Moreover, it has always been an accepted part of the lore that some boys were born like that.* As a matter of fact, my brother and uncle reminded me that Jabo was only one of several sissies in the neighborhood, all of whom claimed that they were "born like that."

THE MUSIC MINISTRY: A MAJOR SOURCE OF THE HOMOPHOBIA

Allow me to begin this section by acknowledging that much of what I have to say is based upon my personal experiences and observations, though I think it will resonate with many of you if music has been a major part of your life as it has been mine—especially the music in the black Baptist church.

First of all, the presence of practicing homosexuals in the music ministries of our churches is the worst-kept secret in the church and a major source and cause of homophobia in the church. It is a well-travelled theory that the reason the music ministry seems to be the source of so much tension and strife in so many of the churches is because the music ministry is the base for Satan. The choir or music ministry, it seems, is afflicted with a preponderance of "hell-raisers" because of the legacy of Lucifer, who was described as a musician: *"The workmanship of your timbrels and pipes was prepared for you on the day you were created"* (Ezekiel 28:13, NKJV). This may be a reference to the instruments played by Lucifer or to his very being.

Whether it refers to his instruments or his being, it seems clear that Lucifer was created as an awesome angelic musician. Scripture tells us that Lucifer did not lose his power or his God-given gifts after his rebellion. He retained his status and power in heaven as the *"anointed cherub"* (verse 14), and on earth he is described as the *"prince of the power of the air, the spirit who now works in the sons of disobedience"* (Ephesians 2:2, NKJV). Music is produced by "airwaves" and Lucifer, as the prince of the air, now uses his gift to influence musicians to behave as *"sons of disobedience"* in ways that do not glorify God.

Lest I be accused of dislike or disrespect for musicians, let me make it clear that I am a lifelong music fan. Music has always been and continues to be a major part of my life. I enjoy and appreciate all genres of music—jazz, blues, R&B, gospel, classical, and even some rap. I attribute this, first, to my roots as a child living in the backyard of downtown Birmingham, Alabama; my friends and I often snuck into the backdoor of the nearby city auditorium (Boutwell) where we saw and heard all types of musicians playing all types of music. One week we might hear the gospel concert featuring the Five Blind Boys of Alabama, the Soul Stirrers. and Mahalia Jackson. The next week it might be an R&B concert with James Brown, Louis Jordan, and the Tympany Five. The next week it could be the blues concert featuring Muddy Waters, B. B. King, and Guitar Slim. One of my lasting memories was that of sitting in the balcony while the whites hurled insults at the black performer Nat King Cole.

As a teenager I was exposed to gospel by my neighbors Andraé and Sandra Crouch, who lived across the street and with whom I walked to school daily in Pacoima, California. Andraé, who recently went home to be with the Lord, became legendary before his departure. As an adult I became an aficionado of "avant-garde" jazz, so much so that I named my first son Coltrane, after jazz giant John Coltrane.

I cite this to indicate that I have had, and continue to have, a lifelong love affair with music and musicians. So my comments here, though based upon my own experiences, might sound familiar, if you have been a lifelong lover of music. First, my observations and comments seem to be consistent with musicians whether in the secular world or in the world of gospel music. The gift of music in many musicians I have observed seems to be accompanied by what I can only describe as an almost idiosyncratic, feminine mystique.

In an almost mystical way, music penetrates the heart and soul as only a woman can, bringing feelings of love, tenderness, and gentleness. Music can bring you joy and exultation, engaging your feet with stomping and your hands with clapping almost unconsciously. Great musicians like the music they create, and exude a sensitivity and tenderness that is closely associated with the softness of a female. Music has the power to entice and seduce one into a realm of fantasy and imagination. Music, whether gospel or secular, has the power to transport listeners to realms beyond the present. The blues can take you down to the ground, and gospel can take you up to the heavens.

I have been struck, however, with the observation of how so many of the most famous male musicians whom I adore and appreciate—some still alive and others who have passed on—exhibited effeminate behaviors or traits. More than a few from both the secular and sacred world were openly gay or bisexual. I don't think I have to risk being sued for slander or libel by naming any of them; but if you are a music fan, I am sure some personalities come to your mind.

So it is not surprising to me, nor should it be to you, that the music ministry of *the average black church is populated with individuals who exhibit effeminate behavior, most of whom I believe are not homosexual.* Candidly speaking, many of them are just the opposite; they are bona fide "skirt chasers," chasing every female in the choir.

We must take great care not to generalize and make assumptions that because an individual's behavior is effeminate that he is necessarily homosexual. Nevertheless, we must acknowledge that the music ministry has become a haven for homosexuals.

The problem and challenge presented to us lies in the fact that there is a high correlation between numerical church growth and music. Any church that wants to grow numerically in our community must have a dynamic music ministry. Moreover, in many churches, large and small, even the pastor himself must be somewhat of a musician, with the ability to "tune" it up in the closing of his sermon. There are some who even believe that if the preacher can't tune—he can't preach! The black preacher's ability to "tear up the house" is closely related to his ability to tune.

It is a sad commentary but no less true. In the traditional black Baptist church, the folks will overlook the preacher's lack of education and training and even his ability to rightly divide the Word—if he can tune!

This overemphasis upon the music ministry, coupled with the preponderance of homosexual musicians, has propelled many of the homosexual choir directors and ministers of music into positions of power and influence that rivals that of the pastor. Oftentimes, the musician has more influence with individual choir members than does the pastor. And, in more than a few places across the country, there are stories where conflict between pastor and musician has led to church splits, with many of the choir members leaving the church to follow the musician.

After splitting the church, these self-appointed gay pastors move across town, organize their own churches, oftentimes debunking the title of "church" and preferring to be known as "ministries" or "centers."

This growing phenomenon has done as much as anything to contribute to the homophobia felt by many in the black church.

Second, it must also be acknowledged that some of those who are homosexual musicians move from the piano to the pulpit. This is evidenced by the highly publicized exposure of some of our most prominent black preachers as practicing homosexuals. Yet, in spite of their exposure, most of them continue in their tenures as pastor because of their popularity.

The popularity of some homosexual musicians has created fear (phobia) in the members of the board of deacons or elders who may disagree with their homosexuality but, recognizing how difficult it is to find good musicians, are afraid to discipline them. This phobia is so real in many churches that homosexual musicians literally hold the churches hostage to their demands, which sometimes includes demanding salaries that rival that of the pastor's. Still others use this phobia to flaunt their homosexual lifestyle with their flaming attire, mannerisms, and insolence toward authority.

This phobia, or fear, is also seen in the reticence or outright refusal of many pastors to preach about the issue of homosexuality, fearing that it will make many in the congregation uncomfortable. Again, this is especially true of some members of the choir who, in their efforts to be supportive of the music ministry, take sides with the musician in spite of his open homosexuality, becoming what the gay community affectionately calls "fag hags" (friends of fags).

The foregoing information, I believe, firmly establishes the presence, practice, and phobia of homosexuality in the black church. We now turn to the question of what to do about it.

CHAPTER

8

What Can the Church Do?

I was reminded rather forcefully by Tim Wilkins, a self-described "former homosexual," that "the Great Commission is to go and make disciples, not heterosexuals" (Wilkins, Cross Ministry).

Wilkins was a participant in the Spitzer study cited earlier. The Spitzer study, you may recall, focused on heterosexual function of those who called themselves "former homosexuals." He says, "It is absurd for churches and/or therapists to try and make the homosexual heterosexual."

In agreement with conservatives, he acknowledges that the Scripture says explicitly that we are to avoid all forms of sexual immorality, which includes homosexuality. However, he remarks, "The opposite of homosexuality is not heterosexuality, but rather holiness." Wilkins says that heterosexuality should never be the church's goal.

Some Christians err in thinking that gay men simply have not met the right woman. Thus, they think it is their job to introduce the gay man to attractive Christian, heterosexual women. Following this same logic, many churches create a singles ministry designed to bring heterosexual singles together under the banner of the church.

Studies have shown, however, overwhelmingly that gay men and women who get married thinking that they will be "cured" fail miserably. Most become "closet gays" operating on the "DL" (down-low), hiding their homosexual behavior from their friends and family. There are more than a few stories told of married Christian men with wives and families, extending even to the pulpit, who have been shamefully exposed as practicing homosexuals (J. L. King, *Living on the Down Low*; Bishop Eddie Long, *Atlanta Journal-Constitution*, December 4, 2011).

Wilkins confesses that during his journey out of homosexuality he made a marvelous discovery—"Jesus Christ is not a means to an end; namely heterosexuality. He is the Alpha and the Omega, the First and the Last, the Beginning and the End. Disciples imitate their Masters. When we focus on making disciples of gays, they will become conformed to the image of the Firstborn Son."

I cite the testimony of this pastor because I believe that it provides a different perspective from which to proceed, and it is with this in mind that I offer some guidelines.

GUIDELINES FOR CONFRONTING HOMOPHOBIA

The following guidelines and principles are developed to help those who believe that the current epidemic requires a proactive response from the church, and want to begin doing so as an individual and as a local church. They represent a balanced approach based upon the information and insight gained from a diligent search of the Scriptures, scientific studies, personal testimonies, and personal experiences of the author.

As iron sharpens iron, may they be used of God as instruments to stir up the gift in each of you, providing you with empowerment to confront the homophobia, and even the more as we see the Day approaching.

BE PRAYERFUL.

As always, as in everything, approach the topic with prayer and the confidence that the Spirit of Truth will guide you in your search and empower you in your efforts.

BE OPEN-MINDED.

Set aside as much as possible all of your prejudices and predispositions about the causes and cures of homosexuality.

BE HONEST.

Acknowledge that, contrary to our beliefs, there is testimonial evidence in most of our own experiences and in the testimonies of others in our communities of the longstanding existence of homosexuality in our communities, in our families, and in our churches as well.

BE INFORMED.

Read and research the literature and studies on homosexuality, including those written by pro-gay activists, and become conversant on the language used by those in the LGBT community. Use the books and articles listed in the bibliography of this book to become better informed.

BE BIBLICAL.

Look at the biblical passages referenced in this book and search for additional interpretations. Use sound hermeneutical principles and develop your own perspective on the subject. Stand firmly on the biblical principle that homosexuality is a sin, but not an unforgivable sin.

BE CLEAR.

Be clear in your teachings that homosexuality is no more abominable than any other sin. Make it clear that forgiveness and restoration are as available to homosexuals as they are to any other repentant sinner.

BE LOVING AND ACCEPTING.

Approach the homosexual with the love of Christ, extending to him the same privileges you would extend to any unsaved person. Accept the person(s) for who they are and do not try to change them from homosexuals to heterosexuals. Accept gay couples, but do not condone or perform gay marriages, as it violates the clear teaching of Scripture that marriage is between a male and a female.

BE CONSISTENT.

Extend to the homosexual the same liberties that you do to the heterosexuals. Do not develop rules of conduct and attire for the homosexual that are not applicable to the heterosexual. Encourage gender-appropriate attire for everyone, especially those serving in ministries with youth.

BE A DISCIPLER.

Be a discipler of every believer whom God directs to your congregation, focusing upon their spirituality rather than their sexuality. Diligently teach new converts to obey the commandments of the Lord Jesus Christ. Trust the Holy Spirit to do the work of sanctification that brings them under submission to the authority of the Word and the biblical teachings on homosexuality.

Epilogue

As indicated in my biography, I was a college professor when I was converted. As such, I valued scholarship highly and looked with disdain upon those in the preaching ministry who had little or no formal training. So when I finally gave in and responded to the call to the ministry I began by acknowledging my own ignorance of the Scriptures, which led me to resign from the university to become a full-time seminarian. Two years into my seminary experience, I was called to the pastorate and given the privilege of organizing a local church fellowship. In deciding what name to give the fellowship, I was led to name it after the practice of the believers in the little town of Berea, to where the apostle Paul fled from his persecutors in Thessalonica. Luke, writing about these persons in Acts, said of them, *"Now the Berean Jews were of more noble character than those in Thessalonica, for they received the message with great eagerness and examined the Scriptures every day to see if what Paul said was true"* (Acts 17:11, NIV).

As a converted scholar, I wanted to organize our church around the principle of being open-minded but not gullible. For the thirty-five years of my tenure in the ministry, I have sought diligently to live by those principles. As such, when I was thrust out of the pastorate to serve as a full-time teaching evangelist and apologist, I approached every doctrinal controversy with an open mind, searching the Scriptures to see what was true. The range and number of controversies to which I was asked to give an opinion became so voluminous that I decided to catalogue them in a book (Burwell, 2004).

More often than I would like to admit, my devotion to behave as a good Berean has led me to conclusions that shattered my own previously held positions. Such, I must admit, has been my experience with this volatile issue. I entered this study with the heartfelt notion expressed in the oft-repeated phrase "a person cannot be born gay"; in other words, I did not believe that there was such thing as a constitutional homosexual. I held this position even as late as the publication of my book just a few years ago.

I was greatly sold out to this position, so much so that when I learned that

President Barack Obama had come out in support of gay unions, I loudly protested, reminding my peers that I had already written a chapter in my book labeling him as a politician "upon whose face the mask of a parishioner did not fit comfortably." I was contemptuous of his explanation that he had a change of mind as a result of his longtime intimacy with gay members of his staff. So it is with more than a little tongue-in-cheek that I now must recant my opinion about his decision.

Like those of the president, my beliefs and practices have "evolved" over a lifetime (see "Obama's Views on Gay Marriage 'Evolving,'" *Washington Post,* June 11, 2011). My evolution, though, has come about not simply as a result of my personal experiences and interactions with gays—though I acknowledge a few—but primarily as a result of my responsibility as a teacher of God's Word.

I am a firm believer not only in the authority of Scripture but also of the sufficiency of Scripture. I believe that all truth is of God and that the Bible is the highest revelation of God. I believe that God has given you and me who are believers the ability to use our minds to evaluate and consider information from a wide range of sources, with the Bible as the standard. As such, scientifically verified or not, it is from God if it is true. Truth, irrespective of its source, as such, must be neither discounted nor dismissed.

Inasmuch as I seek to make the Bible my authority for life and living, allow me to lay out my biblical basis for my change, of which I will elucidate later.

The first is based first upon the paucity of biblical references to homosexuality. I entered this study expecting to find a large number of Scriptures that would clearly enumerate not only the prohibition against homosexuality, but also support for my dogmatism that "a person cannot be born gay."

Instead, after a diligent search of both the Old and the New Testament, I discovered an unsettling small number of passages explicitly addressing the issue of homosexuality. Admittedly, without much study, I had taken the word of my peers, who often surreptitiously cited homosexuality as not simply a sin but an "abomination," implying that it was one more heinous than other sins. My search of the Scriptures revealed, however, that they had erred by failing to take note of the passages where homosexuality is characterized as an abomination, but is done so along with other sins equally abominable.

Take, for example, the most frequently quoted text of Leviticus 18:22, which I discussed earlier; indeed, it explicitly forbids homosexuality: ***"Thou shalt not*** *lie with mankind, as with womankind: it is abomination."* However, it is only one among several "Thou shall nots" in the context. These prohibitions are summarized by saying *"Ye shall ... not commit <u>any</u> of these abominations"* (verse 26). The term is used here in the plural, indicating that it is not the only abomination.

In the New Testament, the most often quoted text is Romans 1, in which homosexuality is a practice among those that *"God gave over to a reprobate mind"* (verse 28). In that text, the term translated "fornication" may rightfully refer to homosexuality. But it should be noted once again that it is only one among many on a list summarized as *"<u>all</u> unrighteousness."* The list goes on to include *"wickedness, covetousness, maliciousness; . . . envy, murder, debate, deceit, malignity, whisperers, backbiters,"* and so forth.

This has led me to the clear conviction that homosexuality is a sin condemned in both the Old and the New Testament. It is, however, no more or any less a sin than are the other sins in the list of vices.

The salient issue of whether or not a person can be born gay is a theological issue. As such, it must be answered based upon the whole counsel of God, not simply those texts that refer explicitly to homosexuality. Herein, we must evaluate and respond accordingly to the pro-gay claim of being constitutionally gay.

From a theological perspective, it may prove helpful to reflect on and remind ourselves of the effects of the Fall. In so doing we should remember that it affected the totality of man's being; everything would, henceforth, begin to behave *unnaturally.* Even the very dust of the ground from which before *naturally* yielded food would now behave *unnaturally* and yield thistles and thorns, making it necessary for him to till the fields for food.

In other words, the entire world and everything that dwells therein—man and beast, fish and fowl, the sea and the land—all fell under the curse of the Fall. Is it reasonable to think that this curse does not extend to the prenatal processes of fertilization, incubation, etc., affecting even natural and unnatural behavior of genes that determine sexual orientation? Is it over-reaching to conclude that this unnatural genetic behavior produces unnatural results, like homosexuality rather than heterosexuality?

Can a person be born gay? My answer is couched in what the Lord Jesus said speaking about the matter of divorce: *"It was not this way in the beginning* (Matthew 19:8). In the beginning, in God's perfect creation, after each day's work, He declared that *"it was good."* In that Edenic state, everything functioned *naturally* in accordance with its intended purpose.

However, after the Fall, nothing would function naturally in accordance with its intended purpose. The judgment of God falls first upon the serpent: *"Cursed are you above all livestock and all wild animals! You will crawl on your belly and you will eat dust all the days of your life"* (Genesis 3:14, NIV).

Immediately after dealing with the serpent, God turns to the woman: *"I will your pains in childbearing very severe; with painful labor you will give birth to children"* (Genesis 3:16, NIV). Is this not an early indication that the very act of childbirth, which was to occur naturally without pain, will henceforth occur unnaturally by being accompanied by pain? Does not this curse at least allow the possibility that all of human sexuality will be negatively affected?

Inasmuch as childbirth will become unnatural, is it a far leap to believe that this will not extend to fertilization and the behavior of genes?

Indeed, then, it is my considered opinion that sin has invaded, polluted, and perverted the natural birth process, resulting in homosexual births; akin to that which has produced hermaphrodites. As such, the church should no longer hold to the longstanding belief that homosexuality cannot be constitutional. To be absolutely clear, the church must recognize the error of the claim that "a person cannot be born gay."

With that being said, I am equally convinced that such births are as uncommon as are hermaphrodites. Concomitantly, then, while we can no longer rush to the judgment that a person cannot be born gay, *we must also take note that the statistics reveal that the overwhelming number of practicing homosexuals are victims of a myriad of societal ills ranging from rape and incest to dysfunctional family structures, to mention but a few.*

The church's phobia coupled with the rapid strides made by the LGBT community has given impetus to the misconception that *all* gays are constitutionally gay. By acknowledging that a small percentage of people may be born gay, the church is free to focus upon the 97 percent who are victimized twice by homosexuality. They are first victimized by the societal malady that led to their homosexuality, and victimized again, by the church's refusal to acknowledge their condition.

As I indicated earlier, our young people are wide open to the influence of the LGBT-controlled media, including the worlds of sports and entertainment. The message of the LGBT heralds the news of individuals who are constitutionally gay, but ignores the statistics showing that *more than 80 percent of black, male homosexuals come from families of female-headed households and/or families where there is a weak male and a dominating female* (Peggy Drexler, *Raising Boys without Men*).

We are not told about the shocking number of females who were victims of sexual abuse as children and, because of this abuse, turned to lesbianism in search of healing. We hear nothing about studies showing that the greatest number of HIV/AIDS patients are from the minority communities with African Americans leading the list, many of whom were homosexuals ("HIV & AIDS among African Americans," Center for Disease Control, May 2015).

One of the underlying principles of sociology, aptly demonstrated in the book of Acts, is that "needs give rise to ministries" (see Acts 6:1-7). The ills being heaped upon our communities provides us with an opportunity, as well as a challenge. Living as we are, in the end times, perhaps more than ever before the church can show the world that in spite of the apparent success and evil spawned by the LGBT community there is yet a balm in Gilead!

I conclude this little study with a few personal notes and reflections that contributed to my interest and subsequent pursuit of this subject. After our ministry tours of three years each in Hartford, Connecticut, and San Antonio, Texas, respectively, my wife and I decided to relocate to a place where we could be near our children and three recently arrived grandchildren living in the Los Angeles area. Through the miraculous leading and provision of the Lord, we were moved into a gated community in the internationally known city of Palm Springs, the "Playground of the Stars." This city is part of a desert community located one hundred miles east of Los Angeles, where many of the retired, rich, and famous live during the winter months.

In the excitement of praising God for this wonderful blessing we somehow missed the fact that for all of the things for which the area is known, it is also known for being one of the largest, per-capita gay communities in the world. The reality of what this portended came upon me, when I was invited, by a person from the rather small nearby black community, to serve as the speaker at a local church commemorating Dr. Martin L. King Day. Sharing the stage with me at this event was the recently elected mayor of the city, who was black and openly gay (I had not met him but had been told these details).

However, I was not quite prepared when we were introduced, and he excitedly responded, "Professor Burwell, is that you?"—doing so with outstretched arms to embrace me. Immediately when he said that, I recognized him. He had been a student of mine twenty years earlier, while in his freshman year, at the university where I taught.

Yet, when he approached me, I unconsciously felt myself recoiling, reluctant to reciprocate. That was the beginning of *my recognition of the homophobia residing inside of me, and the beginning of a resocialization process that lasted for the thirteen years that we lived there.*

I then became aware that our condominium complex of about forty residents consisted of mostly gay couples. Most of the gays who were old, retired, and monogamous had been living together as partners much longer than the brief seven years of mine and my wife's marriage.

Though our contact was limited to the annual association meetings, and a few that occasionally visited the community pool, we experienced nothing different from living in the heterosexual communities than in the afore-mentioned cities. We learned to accept as normal their walking hand in hand, but never did we observe any inappropriate behaviors; nor were we or any of our children visiting us over the years ever approached in an inappropriate sexual manner.

Moreover, on Sunday mornings as we left home en route to our little black church in the neighborhood on the north end of town, I witnessed their faithful attendance at the gay-affirming First Baptist Church of Palm Springs, located just outside the gates of our complex.

Finally, I would be remiss not to acknowledge the openly gay brother of our best friend in the community, with whom we frequently shared dinner accompanied by his partner and a number of other gay couples. In all of our interactions, I was continually impressed with not only their devotion to one another, but also their respect for me and my wife. They did this in spite of the fact that they knew through my writings and my teachings of my opposition to gay unions. Their respect extended even to my practice of praying before meals, each time asking me to bless the food.

Lastly, in an almost providential way, as I was making copies of this manuscript at the office of my apartment complex, the ink cartridge ran dry. I asked one of the managers to replace it; as he did so, I noticed him showing more than a little interest, prompting me to ask him if he was interested in the topics. Then, tearfully, he said, "I have been struggling with this my entire life. I don't know why anyone would think that this is a choice. I was born and reared in the Midwest where homosexuality was looked upon as deviant and devilish. The pain it has caused has led me almost to the brink of suicide."

This man's face is clearly before me as I close this manuscript. The pain so evident on his face served to reaffirm the conclusion of my diligent prayers and scholarship. Homosexuality is indeed constitutional for some, and for most of these it is like a never-ending dark cloud over their lives.

As such, it reaffirmed also the great need that we in the church have to reevaluate our beliefs and our behaviors with regards to the issue of homosexuality, with the recognition that, irrespective of the cause of homosexuality or whether it begins at birth or sometimes later, our mission is the same: *"make disciples of all the nations"* (Matthew 28:19, NKJV).

It is my prayer that this book will prove helpful in preparing and prompting those of us in the black church, who are well-acquainted with the pain of disenfranchisement, to confront homophobia not with *"a spirit of fear; but of power, and of love, and of a sound mind"* (2 Timothy 1:7, NKJV).

Appendix

The process of conducting a survey among us proved to be much more challenging than I anticipated. The first challenge I encountered was that of getting churches to participate and respond in a timely manner. Then there were more than a few participants whose responses indicated that they were either confused or simply disinterested; therefore, their responses had to be eliminated. I recognize that this is a very small sampling; nevertheless, I believe it is a representative sampling of the attitudes of black Baptists across the country.

Because I am currently living in Knoxville, Tennessee, most of the respondents were from this region. There were eight churches responding to the survey; four were from the Knoxville region, and included teachers attending a seminar in the Knoxville District Baptist Educational Association. There were two churches from the Midwest, one from the South, and one from the West. The participating churches were as follows:

- BETHANY BAPTIST CHURCH *of* WEST LOS ANGELES
  Dr. L. A. Kessee, *Pastor-Teacher*
  Los Angeles, CA

- GREATER MT. OLIVE BAPTIST CHURCH
  Rev. Ray Douglas, *Pastor-Teacher*
  Oklahoma City, OK

- KNOXVILLE DISTRICT BAPTIST MISSIONARY *and* EDUCATIONAL ASSOCIATION
  Dr. Joe B. Maddox, *Moderator*
  Knoxville, TN

- NEW HOPE MISSIONARY BAPTIST CHURCH
  Dr. Joe B. Maddox, *Pastor-Teacher*
  Knoxville, TN

- PAYNE AVENUE MISSIONARY BAPTIST CHURCH
  Rev. Richard S. Brown Jr., *Pastor-Teacher*
  Knoxville, TN

- ST. LUKE BAPTIST CHURCH
  John Bowden, *Pastor-Teacher*
  Birmingham, AL

- MOUNT PLEASANT MISSIONARY BAPTIST CHURCH
  Rev. L. Henderson Bell, *Pastor-Teacher*
  Kansas City, MO

- ST. JOHN MISSIONARY BAPTIST CHURCH
  Rev. Charles Lomax, *Pastor-Teacher*
  Alcoa, TN

- TABERNACLE MISSIONARY BAPTIST CHURCH
  Elder Christopher Battle Sr., *Pastor-Teacher*
  Knoxville, TN

CONFRONTING HOMOPHOBIA IN THE BLACK CHURCH
DR. BILL BURWELL JR., AUTHOR
Black Church Attitudinal Survey

Please identify yourself by checking the box to the left of the appropriate categories below:

☐ Male   ☐ Female

☐ Heterosexual ☐ Homosexual   ☐ Bi-sexual   ☐ Lesbian

☐ Under Age 20   ☐ Age 20-40   ☐ Over Age 40

```
1------2-------3-------4-------5-------6-------7--------8-------9------10
⊢—Strongly Disagree————————— Agree ———————— Strongly Agree —⊣
```

*Using the above scale, please write the number that best expresses
your agreement or disagreement with the following:*

_____ 1. According to the Bible, homosexuality is an unforgivable sin.

_____ 2. According to the Bible, homosexuality is a sin, but no greater

than any other sin.

_____ 3. Homosexuality is learned behavior and therefore a choice.

_____ 4. I knew someone who acted like a homosexual before the age

of five and everyone agreed that the child was born that way.

_____ 5. A person cannot be born gay.

_____ 6. Persons who live a gay lifestyle cannot be saved.

_____ 7. A born-again Christian cannot be a practicing homosexual.

SURVEY RESULTS

*The total number of respondents were 315
and some of them did not respond to all of the questions.*

1. ACCORDING TO THE BIBLE, HOMOSEXUALITY IS AN UNFORGIVABLE SIN.

204 Strongly Disagree   46 Agree   65 Strongly Agree

2. ACCORDING TO THE BIBLE, HOMOSEXUALITY IS A SIN, BUT NO GREATER THAN ANY OTHER SIN.

71 Strongly Disagree   82 Agree   164 Strongly Agree

3. HOMOSEXUALITY IS LEARNED BEHAVIOR AND THEREFORE A CHOICE.

75 Strongly Disagree   51 Agree   149 Strongly Agree

4. I KNEW SOMEONE WHO ACTED LIKE A HOMOSEXUAL BEFORE THE AGE OF FIVE AND EVERYONE AGREED THAT THE CHILD WAS BORN THAT WAY.

163 Strongly Disagree   93 Agree   62 Strongly Agree

5. A PERSON CANNOT BE BORN GAY.

84 Strongly Disagree   74 Agree   122 Strongly Agree

6. PERSONS WHO LIVE A GAY LIFESTYLE CANNOT BE SAVED.

225 Strongly Disagree   38 Agree   33 Strongly Agree

7. A BORN-AGAIN CHRISTIAN CANNOT BE A PRACTICING HOMOSEXUAL.

107 Strongly Disagree   84 Agree   83 Strongly Agree

OBSERVATIONS

• One hundred fifty-five individuals said in response to question number 4 that they "knew someone whom everyone agreed was gay at an early age." However, 196 respondents said in response to question number 5 that "a person cannot be born gay." *This gives credence to the thesis that the black church violates the law of non-contradiction.*

• Almost 20 percent of those surveyed believe that the Bible teaches that homosexuality is an unforgivable sin, an indication that more teaching on the subject needs to be done.

• Almost 25 percent of the respondents believe that homosexuality is a greater sin than others, perhaps because of the teachings that single it out as an "abomination."

• One-third or 35 percent of respondents believe that homosexuality is learned behavior and therefore a choice.

• More than 70 percent of the respondents to statement number 6 indicated that "gays can be saved." Significantly, however, 50 percent of the respondents to question number 7 said that "individuals living the gay lifestyle, such as same-sex couples, are not saved."

Bibliography

Alexander, Richard. "Parental Manipulation Theory." *The Desert Sun* newspaper, September 21, 2000.

Bailey, Sherwin D. *Homosexuality and the Western Tradition.* London: Longmans, Green and Co., 1955.

Bao, Ai-Min, and Dick F. Swaab. "Sexual Differentiation of the Human Brain: Relation to Gender Identity, Sexual Orientation and Neuropsychiatric Disorders." *Frontiers in Neuroendocrinology* 32 (2011).

Barnett, Walter. *Homosexuality and the Bible: An Interpretation.* Wallingford, PA: Pendle Hill Publishing, 1979.

Bearman, Peter, and Hannah Bruckner. "Opposite Sex Twin Study." *Journal of Sociology,* vol. 107 (May 2001): 1179-1205.

Boswell, John. *Christianity, Social Tolerance, and Homosexuality.* Chicago: University of Chicago Press, 1980.

Brownlee, William H. *Word Biblical Commentary.* Waco: Word Books, 1986.

Burwell, William. *ShoNuff: Confronting the Controversies.* Oklahoma City: Tate Publishing, 2004.

Denominational Statements on Homosexuality. (Religion.link.org., Associated Press, Times Research).

Dorner, G., and F. Docke. Paper on "Homo– and Hypersexuality in Rats with Hypothalmic Lesions." Conducted at the Institute of Experimental Indoor Endocrinology at Humboldt University, Berlin, Germany, 1969.

Featherstone, David. "Fruit Fly Study and Homosexuality" (University of Illinois). *Science Daily* (December 10, 2007).

Gates, Gary. Gallup Poll. Princeton, NJ. www.gallup.com.

Gooren, Louis. "The Biology of Human Psychosexual Differentiation." *Hormones and Behavior* (2006).

Grady, J. Lee. "How I Know Jonathan and David Weren't Gay." *Charisma,* June 2013.

Halpern, David. *One Hundred Years of Homosexuality.* New York: Routledge, Chapman & Hall, 1990.

Hamer, Dean. "Gay Gene Study." *Journal of Science* (July 1993).

Hooker, Evelyn. "The Adjustment of the Male Overt Homosexual." *Journal of Projective Techniques,* vol. 21 (1957): 18-31.

Layton, Lynne. "In Defense of Gender Ambiguity," by Jessica Benjamin. *Gender & Psychoanalysis,* vol. 1, no. 1 (1996).

LeVay, Simon. *A Difference in Hypothalamic Structure between Homosexual and Heterosexual Men.* San Diego, CA: Salk Institute, 1991.

Money, John. *Gay, Straight, and In-between.* New York and Oxford: Oxford University Press, 1988.

National Council of Churches, USA. *Yearbook of American and Canadian Churches, 2011.* Nashville, TN: Abingdon Press, 2011.

Nimmons, David. "Sex and the Brain." *Discover Magazine* (March 1994).

Pillard, Richard, and Michael Bailey. "A Genetic Study of Male Sexual Orientation." Boston, MA: Boston University School of Medicine, 1991.

Roach, John. "Lesbians Respond Differently to Sweat and Urine." A study conducted in the Karolinska Institutet in Stockholm, Sweden; published September 2005.

Rosner, Fred. *Maimonides' Commentary on the Mishnah, Sanhedrin.* New York: Sepher-Hermon Press, 1981.

Scanzoni, Letha, and Virginia Ramey Mollenkott. *Is the Homosexual My Neighbor? Another Christian View.* London: SCM Press, 1978.

Schenker, J. G. "Human Reproduction: Jewish Perspectives" (1987). *Gynecological Endocrinology* (November 2013).

Spitzer, Robert. "Ex-Gay Study." Conducted at Columbia University in New York, 2001.

———. "Gays Can Change." *Archives of Sexual Behavior* (National Association for Research Therapy of Homosexuality), vol. 32, no. 5 (October 2003): 403-417.

Swaab, D. F., and M. A. Hoffman. "A Study of the Human Brain: Heterosexuals and Homosexuals." Conducted at the Graduate School of Neurosciences, Amsterdam, December 6, 1994.

Tag Archives: blaquebigayministers (Tag Archives: blaquebigayministers).

Thorp, John. "The Social Construction of Homosexuality." Critical response to Michael Foucault. A lecture delivered to the Classical Association of Canada in May 1990.

Transas City. "The Transgender Brain." www.transascity.org.

Turner, Charles. "Same-Sex Gender among U.S. Adults." *Public Opinion Quarterly*, vol. 69, no. 3 (May 2005).

Ukleja, Michael P. *Homosexuality and the Bible.* Bellingham, WA: Victor Books, 1990.

White, Mel. *What the Bible Says—And Doesn't Say—about Homosexuality.* Lynchburg, VA: Soulforce, 2005.

Wilkins, Tim. More than Words Conference. Cross Ministry. www.crossministry.org.

Young, Pamela. *Feminist Theology/Christian Theology: In Search of Method.* Eugene, OR: Wipf and Stock Publishers, 2000.

CPSIA information can be obtained
at www.ICGtesting.com
Printed in the USA
LVHW032252160223
739728LV00014B/983

9 781939 225542